T0296047

Oracle Business Intelligence and Essbase Solutions Guide

Oracle Business Intelligence and Essbase Solutions Guide

Rosendo Abellera • Lakshman Bulusu

CRC Press
Taylor & Francis Group
Boca Raton   London   New York

CRC Press is an imprint of the
Taylor & Francis Group, an **Informa** business

AN AUERBACH BOOK

CRC Press
Taylor & Francis Group
6000 Broken Sound Parkway NW, Suite 300
Boca Raton, FL 33487-2742

© 2017 by Taylor & Francis Group, LLC
CRC Press is an imprint of Taylor & Francis Group, an Informa business

No claim to original U.S. Government works

Printed on acid-free paper
Version Date: 20161108

International Standard Book Number-13: 978-1-4822-3407-7 (Hardback)

Visit the Taylor & Francis Web site at
http://www.taylorandfrancis.com

and the CRC Press Web site at
http://www.crcpress.com

Printed and bound in the United States of America by Sheridan

Dedication

I dedicate this book to the loving memory of my mother, Smt. B. Sita, who has always been an inspiration to me in my writing and has always encouraged me to write more. Thank you, Mom. Your words will always be a guiding light to me as I move from one book to another.

– Lakshman Bulusu

I dedicate my first book to the memory of my father, Dr. Rosito Pimentel Abellera, who, as a man of a few words, whispered in my ear to "Go for it" when he bid me farewell as a young man stepping out onto the great big scary world on my own.

Dad, you instilled in me the faith to make it through thick and thin and inspired me to always believe. How I wish I had told you in person while I had the chance that I greatly admired your character, strength, and courage. We all miss you so much. Your love for life lives in our hearts and minds as we step out to seek new adventures and endeavors.

– Rosendo Abellera

Contents

Foreword

William Heenan

Analytics has been around in some form for many years. Even before the advent of computers. The concepts are the same and smart people have known this their entire lifetime. Today, it's a matter of looking at one's business and figuring out how to be more efficient. Thousands of years ago, cavemen looked for tracks, studied feeding patterns of animals, and were able to narrow down the best place to catch that tasty wild boar.

While I am not saying that the ancient caveman could develop an advanced system, he was able to put many pieces of information together to draw conclusions. While his end goal was to find an animal to eat, he had to look at lots of key facts. He looked at not only attributes about what he was tracking (e.g, tracks, depth of track, distance between, etc. . . .), but also weather facts, plants facts (e.g., types of plants, how much was eaten by animals, any broken branches, etc. . . .). He also worried about logistics, which all of the previous information played into. How big was the animal, which could be determined by track size, stride length, food consumption, and how many trees/branches were broken. He also worried about weather. If this animal is too big, how am I going to drag it home? Do I have access to friends to help me carry it? How much of the kill will I have to share?

Today we ask the same questions and see the relationships in this wealth of information. Today the questions might be more in line with moving a company's headquarters from one state to another. The details lay in many areas to truly answer the question. Employee counts, floor space, logistics to move it all, tax breaks, general business taxes, employee-retention issues, and on and on. The CEO would have to look at all of these factors—costs, savings, logistics, uprooting families, and more—to make the best decisions. Just as the ancient caveman decided if the wild boar was worth the risk, the modern CEO has to consider very similar tidbits of information to make the right decision.

So how does the modern day caveman (CEO) use analytics to make the decision to catch the wild boar? He needs to not only look at each piece of information but also find a way to bring all of this information together as one cohesive set of data. He must conceptually (and logically) understand all of the business's data and the inherent relationships between them. Our modern day caveman can be greatly aided by a blueprint or model. Consider the following approach:

The first step in building a model for a business is to actually identify the lines of business that make it up. For our modern-day business, these may include accounting, human resources, supply, logistics, sales, and so forth, or whatever else the organization's needs entail. While all organizations have similar lines of business such as accounting, human resources, and recruiting, each organization will have others that make it unique. Identification and empowerment of personnel within each line of business fuels the strategy for determining a business's information needs.

Then for each business area, you must determine the main entities and attributes that describe and make up that business area. This conceptual and logical exercise is where business and technology begin to converge as the entities and attributes identify the business data that is required which, in turn, can then "fuel" your analysis. It is critical to identify all of the attributes and relationships, although this may evolve in an iterative manner according to the reporting and analytical needs. You can continue to grow each of the business areas with entities and attributes and also start building relationships between them as your business grows or changes. This approach will allow the data warehouse to be built out and grow as additional reporting needs are identified over time.

Thus, with a data model the proper "translation" and evolution from business concept to technology is set into motion and can be captured with an enterprise data model. With this model of the data foundation, a new data-centric application or system using that data can be properly developed. This "blueprint" is the secret to a successful implementation for analytics.

While there are advanced systems and mathematical theories behind modeling, a good modeler is like an artist, having a vision of the business and creative yet practical ways to bring the information needs together. Having been in the business for several decades, I have come to realize that this type of person is hard to come by—a resource that has both business acumen and technical know-how. Unfortunately, books and material that address this topic—both from a high-level and a detailed view of proper implementation—are extremely scarce. A book such as this would help to guide and frame the proper thinking and approach.

In their book, Rosendo Abellera and Lakshman Bulusu have captured that. You begin with chapters that address and properly categorize reporting and analytics at the high, strategic level. Later chapters go into greater detail to help guide you through a certain frame of thought and focus that is data centric. Their book provides both a strategic and tactical framework. It provides a wealth of information about data warehousing (DW) and business intelligence (BI) even for an experienced resource—as if a personal mentor and expert on DW and BI is available at your fingertips for the subject area. All the while, the book keeps in focus and continually reiterates the secret guide—the blueprint, if you will—for successful implementation; that is, the proper data model.

With over 25 years each of direct experience in the industry, the authors remind us of what works out in the field and how the basics can and will extend success into the next generation of BI and analytics. With the proper foundation established by best practices, we can now evolve into related areas that we have longed dreamed of conquering such as predictive analytics, artificial intelligence, and even machine learning. So even for our modern-day caveman, the CEO, analytics is continually evolving and perhaps finally providing the right or even better capabilities. We thank and applaud our authors for "sharpening our tools."

Happy hunting.

William Heenan is the Director of Analytics at Mythics, Inc., a large award-winning and certified Oracle Platinum partner. Bill has been in the industry for over 30 years, with experiences around Analytics, Business Intelligence, Decision Support Systems, data architecture, and database design for 25 of those years. He has been a consultant to numerous customers, including commercial, federal, state, and local governments. Bill has also had a chance to work with some of the industry's pioneers. He is a veteran of the U.S. Marine Corps. When not working he spends time with family and friends, which is very important to him. He also has been known to run a marathon or hit the links on a lazy summer day.

Preface

I feel honored to have served in Intelligence for the United States. After I spent nearly a decade in the U.S. Armed Forces, there was no shortage of accolades and gratuity expressed by family, friends, and strangers alike to make me indeed feel thanked and appreciated.

So when I heard the joke and felt the sarcasm for the first time, it left me in deep thought, wondering what it really meant. Whenever I was asked what I did in the service, I would answer, "Military intelligence." Jokingly, the response was almost always, "Isn't that an oxymoron?" It took a little getting used to, but after a while it always resulted in a chuckle. Quite clever, it was a running joke that stuck with me.

When I left the service, I started out in my new career in software development and information technology in the civilian world. My software career grew in and around data-centric application development, and during this time, surprisingly, a whole new exciting industry and market had begun to emerge in intelligence and analytics which drew some parallels to what I had been doing in the military and—what do you know—they called it *Business Intelligence*. I had to chuckle. Nevertheless, I dove into this new discipline of knowledge management and intelligence head first. I was determined to master it. I was proud of my newfound endeavor and actually felt gallant about its lofty goals of pursuing knowledge and intelligence, as I had similarly done in the military. Surely there was no way that the oxymoron joke could apply. Could it?

But then I started to observe something quite dismaying. It seemed that in pursuit of business intelligence, organizations would do things that were actually counterproductive to business—things that would actually *cost* them valuable time and money. If business's focus is to make a profit, these crazy situations or SNAFUs (to borrow a humorous acronym used in the military to describe chaotic situations that are problematic and full of issues but, nevertheless, seems to be the normal state of affairs) quickly run opposite of the goal and intention and could actually destroy an organization.

> *SNAFU (Situation Normal, All Fouled Up): A confused, disorganized or muddled situation that is regarded as normal operating procedure.*

I thought "Could these SNAFUs really be happening in the lofty world of business intelligence?"

For decades now, various technologies and approaches have been tried and proven to identify a clear path as the best practice for building a complete, holistic Business Intelligence (BI) and data warehousing (DW) solution. Yet for all the strides that we have made, organizations still attempt to deliver a solution based on limited to no knowledge. Undoubtedly, without any methodology to guide the team through the complex process, it is difficult to weed out what is unnecessary from what is necessary—moreover, from what is crucial or vital—for a successful delivery of the solution. From my point of view as a practitioner, I regularly witnessed the prevalence of chaotic situations and began to form some classifications around these SNAFUs. Let's take a lighthearted look at some of these. Unfortunately, some reading this might just recognize these situations as their current procedure—and they may not be able to laugh about it wholeheartedly.

1. *The "On-The-Job Training" SNAFU:* In this elusive situation, inexperienced resources use the project to learn what they should have already known or what you expected them to have already known. To avoid this situation, bring in experts early on, even during the process of interviewing, to ensure that resources hired have the necessary basic skillset and talent to be successful.
2. *The "Buzzwords" SNAFU:* This situation is when authoritative titles and buzzwords are hurled around, provide the appearance of actual knowledge and expertise—but appearing is as far as it gets. In this situation, the semblance of expertise without real experience creates a dilemma. An expert practitioner not only "talks the talk" but also "walks the walk." This is the value add that every potential customer should seek and demand.
3. *The "Busy Work" SNAFU:* This sets in when the team is assigned tasks that appear to be important and relevant to the project but actually are not. In this SNAFU, the perpetrators want to ensure that the "busy work" activity is always visible, because appearance and perception is valued above real tasks and crucial work. To the experienced, this activity can be clearly differentiated from productivity. In this situation, expertise is needed to identify and assign real deliverables.

4. *The "Covering All Bases" SNAFU:* This is very similar to the "Busy Work" SNAFU, in that a lot of work is done to make it seem that a solution is actually being created. The major difference is that there is a lot of work being assigned and done from all directions in an attempt to cover all bases that might be deemed important to the inexperienced. This leads to a trap that ends up with each and every issue becoming a "priority" or an "emergency." This situation usually ends up with your resources focused on unnecessary objectives. Similarly, in this situation, an expert is needed to "cut out the noise."

5. *The "Jack of All Trades, Master of None" SNAFU:* This situation occurs when the project leaders are knowledgeable in many areas but lack expertise in the specialized field of DW and BI implementation. Without clear guidance on deep issues, the team and project are catapulted into SNAFU #1 as unexperienced team members are left to fend for themselves and the project essentially becomes on-the-job training. This situation can actually be quickly remedied if the perpetrator seeks subject matter expertise to cover knowledge gaps.

6. *The "Let's Throw More Resources At It" SNAFU:* Probably the most futile and misleading concept is when more resources are arbitrarily added and deemed as a solution. I experienced this situation first-hand where this notion was taken a step further. A newly hired executive came up with a "brilliant idea" for saving money and actually replace seasoned, experienced professionals with lots of inexpensive (but inexperienced) resources. Unfortunately, the real underlying problem was that there weren't enough experienced personnel—and that move virtually wiped out any expertise that the organization may have had. Years later, as expected, this move by the executive resulted in the dissolution of that organization. In this situation, having more resources was not the answer; providing the right resources was. Unfortunately, they learned the hard way that there is no substitute for experience and focusing on quality—not quantity—may have saved them.

Unfortunately, these are based on true stories, so identities have been hidden to protect these perpetrators and masters of SNAFU. Keep in mind that with the help of expert practitioners armed with solid best practices, Business Intelligence need not become an oxymoron.

So there you have it—a humorous take on some troubling situations and styles that may be encountered as a practitioner out in the field as organizations dismiss the difficulties involved in building complex BI and analytical systems and solution. It would seem obvious that expertise and experience is needed to help chop through this jungle of technological mess and clear a path to success with a solid plan based on best practices.

A BI and analytics solution, because of its complexity and many components is not the type of project to begin experimenting with—even if the resource is experienced in a related software or IT field. We have encountered it time and time again: Attempting to create a complex system with no experience or guidance almost always leads to a path of rework down the road or, even worse, to a complete disaster in which nothing is delivered after a great deal of time and money is spent. Or even worse, as previously mentioned, it leads to the demise of your organization. In situations where your organization's success—or even survival—is at stake, you would clearly demand experience and expertise.

So with a love and passion for my chosen discipline and career, I had a new mission. Basically, I wanted to share some of the successes that I had experienced in my long career and provide a basic approach and methodology for others to follow. My first step in attempting this endeavor was to figure out exactly how to get it all down in print—enter Mr. Lakshman Bulusu. I had met Lakshman through a mutual friend who was also a long-time practitioner of DW and BI, and together we all shared a love for this field that married the best of business and technology together. But it was Mr. Bulusu, who had previously written seven technical books dealing with Oracle that served as the catalyst to this endeavor. It was a match made in business intelligence heaven where theory and academics partnered with extensive, practical hands-on experience. It all came together here in this book.

– Rosendo Abellera

We chose our subject with plans to offer a real solution to a prevalent problematic issue that we have encountered in several occasions. I, in fact, was a player in one of the first major projects to try to put all the components of the tool suite all together. It is a subject that even the most advanced and experienced practitioner would find daunting, mainly because of the popularity of the tool as a standalone solution and the integration that is needed for a holistic system. In our industry, there are now simply so many tools to provide and deliver an analytical system and solution with the myriad of vendors and all their offerings of tools and technologies all professing to be the best generically—without reference to the best fit for the function sought. Claims of a one-size-fits-all solution should actually be a red flag to practitioners, who know well that there are no magic solutions that can provide a case of plug-and-play in which software is simply installed and you're off to solution nirvana.

This book was written from a practitioner's point of view, based on experiences collected through several decades of extensive hands-on experience. It is our goal that, by heeding the advice provided, you can avoid some common pitfalls that form a barrier to success. Our attempt in this book is to try to help you by providing a framework that actually works. We highlight a central theme throughout the book as best practice and refer to it as the "secret sauce" to being able to successfully deliver a solution. It is our hope that we can provide the answers and resolve the issues that you may even be encountering right now.

We reveal the key to successfully implementing a data-centric application and system such as BI. We show how by taking the time to first tackle the design and architecture of the data foundation, you can then plan and implement the rest of the system accordingly. It is similar to building a house: the foundation must be designed properly first and then built according to the design. Without this attention to detail and process, the house may easily collapse. So it is with building a complex technological system such as a BI solution. Doing it the wrong way almost always takes a lot longer (because of rework) than if done with proper planning and getting it right from the beginning. Your project or environment need not repeat the failures and issues that we have previously identified as avoidable situations.

We share our proven concept and method used for this endeavor, forged by decades of experience; providing you, the practitioner, a guideline and blueprint for success. Consider the recommendations forwarded in this book for establishing a firm data foundation for your downstream BI and analytical applications. We'll show you how the logical model will provide the "blueprint" necessary to understand to identify and build the right data foundation for your downstream BI and analytical solution. We urge you to avoid the SNAFUs that can plague your project and by all means, we ask that you please do not let *Business Intelligence* be an oxymoron.

But overall, we hope you enjoy and find this book useful.

– Rosendo Abellera
– Lakshman Bulusu

Acknowledgments

First of all, I thank all the readers of my previous books, whose feedback in some form or other has helped me in improving the quality of content in my successive books.

I thank my lovely wife Anuradha and my twins Pranav and Pranati for their patience and cooperation during the period of writing of this book.

I thank Mr. John Wyzalek of CRC Press, the CRC editorial and publishing team, and Mr. Theron Shreve of DerryField Publishing Services for their coordinated help in making this book a reality.

I thank Mr. Rosendo Abellera, my co-author, for writing this book with me. Your expertise on on-the-job Oracle BI holistic solution implementation has enriched the content of this book.

– Lakshman Bulusu

First and foremost, I wanted to thank God for the blessings in my life—that is, my family. To my loving mother Violeta and my supportive siblings Roselito, Roselyn (my counselor and confidant), Roswel, and Ross, I thank you so much for all your patience.

To my wonderful wife, Annie (and family), I thank you for your patience and understanding. To my precious children, Alex, Tori, and Angelica, I thank you for your love. You have changed my life to always inspire to do good and to strive to be a better person.

I thank John Wyzalek and Theron Shreve and their staff for making my first book a reality. A special thank you goes to Lakshman Bulusu, my co-author and friend, who was instrumental in opening up a whole new world of writing for me. May this be merely the beginning of many other collaborations.

Last but not least, a long overdue thanks to Mr. Steven D. Staller of Boca Raton, Florida, who, 25 years ago, gave a young vet a much-needed break into what would become a distinguished career in software technology.

– Rosendo Abellera

About the Authors

Lakshman Bulusu is a Senior Oracle Consultant with 23 years of experience in the fields of Oracle RDBMS, SQL, PL/SQL, EDW/BI/EPM, and Oracle-related Java. As an Enterprise-level data warehouse, and business intelligence solution architect/technical manager in the ORACLE RDBMS space, he focused on a best-fit solution architecture and implementation of the Oracle Industry Data Model for telecom. He has worked  for major clients in the pharma/healthcare, telecom, financial (banking), retail, and media industry verticals, with special emphasis on cross-platform heterogeneous information architecture and design. He has published eight books on Oracle and related technologies, all published in the United States, as well as four books on English poetry. He serves on the development team of qteria.com and Qteria Big Data Analytics.

Mr. Bulusu holds a bachelor of science degree in mathematics with honors and a bachelor of engineering (computer science and engineering). He is OCP-certified and holds an Oracle Masters credential. He was selected as a FOCUS Expert for his research briefs titled "Raising your 'SIQ' (Social Intelligence Quotient): 5 Key Business Indicators," "Raising your 'BIQ' (Business Intelligence Quotient): 5 Things Your Company Can Do NOW," and "High-Fives for an Innovative HR Strategy" on FOCUS.com. He has written a host of technical articles and spoken at major Oracle conferences in the United States and abroad. He can be reached at balakshman@gmail.com.

From military intelligence to business intelli-gence, **Rosendo Abellera** has made a lifelong career out of utilizing data as a critical asset. His early career in software development began with several commercial software packages across various industries and business areas, includ-ing work order management, telecom billing, prescription refill, and even voter registration. This extensive hands-on experience of develop-ing data-driven applications has contributed  heavily to his expertise and proven, successful approach to Business Intelligence (BI) and Analytics solutions development.

As an early adopter and pioneer of BI coupled with modern data warehousing (DW) approaches and technologies, he has successfully architected DW and BI solutions from the ground up for leading companies, including AAA, Comcast, John Hancock Financial, Koch Industries, LexisNexis, Mercury Systems, and State Street Bank. Additionally, Rosendo has consulted a multitude of leading organizations across various industries both in the government and commercial realm. As a DW and BI Subject Matter Expert (SME) and proven success-ful practitioner, he has held key management positions to establish the DW and BI practices of several major, prolific consulting organizations. A consum-mate entrepreneur, he has founded DW and BI firms including a former Oracle Partner as well as a Big Data Analytics company.

Rosendo is a graduate of the University of Nebraska at Omaha and the Defense Language Institute. Moreover, he is a veteran of the U.S. Air Force where he served worldwide as a cryptologist, intelligence analyst, and linguist for several languages. He received commendations for his service including for the direct support of Operation Desert Shield at the National Security Agency (NSA).

Chapter 1

Introduction

In This Chapter

1.1 Introduction

A multitude of companies have now chosen to use business intelligence (BI) and analytics. The general goal is that somehow, BI will allow them to gain insight and knowledge into the data contained within their corporate systems. With this, companies armed with the necessary technologies and tools can address the executive, management, and user reporting and analysis needs of the organization in dealing with visibility and analysis to their corporate data.

With the proliferation of vendors specializing in BI and analytics, it is common to find several tools being used by an organization. Sometimes, you can even find several BI tools being thrown together in an attempt to provide a complete, holistic BI solution for users at all levels and facets of their business. Indeed, one of the major goals when implementing a BI solution is to provide reporting and analytics for the entire enterprise. Most recently, some vendors have successfully made available packaged BI applications that try to provide a complete set of analytics and also provide full-featured platforms for reporting. This book will examine the functional features of a BI and analytics application and will also even discuss the architecture and design of the technical structures that enable the objects (i.e., reports and dashboards).

1.2 A Basic Business Need

In the corporate world, there is a need to have enterprise-class reporting and analytics through a single integrated and trusted source to access vital data and information. Moreover, there is a need for visibility into and access to the data from the main systems to address the organization's prevalent topics, such as (among others):

- Revenue and cost opportunities
- Improved leverage in negotiations
- Accountability and compliance to corporate policies
- Business unit activity
- Strategic and planning initiatives

So then what exactly is this "magic" tool for the corporate decision maker? To some, the solution lies in BI. Organizations look to BI solutions and resources for building the proper solution and providing enterprise-class BI reporting and analytics. The goal for many is to gain, for example:

- Improved business decision making with greater visibility and transparency into transactional data coming from a known, consistent single source for decision making based on facts
- Elimination or limitation of custom, on-the-fly manual development of repetitive reports:
  - Automatically prepare and deliver data from a single source of the truth
  - Eliminate redundant sources of reporting
  - Eliminate silos of reporting from personalized sources or outdated applications
- Implementation of best practices for all business units and activity across the organization, with standard processes of reporting supported by analytics to monitor and gauge report effectiveness
- Implementation of a flexible reporting and analytics management architecture that can grow with business requirements

- Centralized pool of knowledge surrounding an organization's reporting and analytics tools, reducing maintenance and support costs related to the upkeep of various other standalone tools

But behind this "magic" tool for decision making is a complex and often confused system. So let's start with a definition of *business intelligence*.

1.3 What Is Business Intelligence?

Business intelligence in today's BI and analytics landscape can mean many things to many people. Researching sources for any formal definition will yield any number of definitions or meanings. To some people, BI deals with reporting. To others, it is strictly analytics. Then again to others, it includes both types and categories of information. Perhaps they are all correct. But no matter the mechanism or tool used, BI funnels down to a common single notion: having these systems will enable a person or organization to make better, or more effective, business decisions. The two definitions shown below were taken from the corresponding links referred to alongside each. Indeed, both refer to BI being used to "help make business decisions" and "enable more effective strategic, tactical, and operational insights and decision-making." That is the ultimate goal. So what facilitates that capability?

> Business intelligence (BI) is a technology-driven process for analyzing data and presenting actionable information to help corporate executives, business managers and other end users make more informed business decisions. BI encompasses a variety of tools, applications and methodologies that enable organizations to collect data from internal systems and external sources, prepare it for analysis, develop and run queries against the data, and create reports, dashboards and data visualizations to make the analytical results available to corporate decision makers as well as operational workers. (*Source:* http://searchdatamanagement. techtarget.com/definition/business-intelligence)
> Business intelligence (BI) is an umbrella term that includes the applications, infrastructure and tools, and best practices that enable access to and analysis of information to improve and optimize decisions and performance. (*Source:* http://www.gartner.com/it-glossary/ business-intelligence-bi/)

The definitions mention a set of applications, technologies, methodologies, processes, architectures, and the like to explain what BI is. Each definition can allude to a technical capability or even an actual special infrastructure and architecture. Indeed, as implementers and developers of BI solutions, we know that there are specialized skills and knowledge for delivering this special type of system.

This book will explore those applications, technologies, and architectures. Moreover, we will use as an example the Oracle Business Intelligence Enterprise Edition (OBIEE) suite and discuss how, properly used, it can provide the right platform for reporting and analytics.

1.4 Why BI?

From a business context, it is tougher than ever to achieve a competitive advantage with the prevalence of tools and technologies accessible to everyone. The key is to find the right tools and technology. There are few innovations available that can truly offer a breakthrough. Competing on analytical capabilities is one very important and powerful way to break through, sustain advantage over time/economic cycles, and effectively outsmart and out-execute the competition.

Achieving competitive advantage in today's world is vital to a business's growth and well-being. Every decision can greatly affect an organization. For this reason, decision making based on facts at all levels of the enterprise has become increasingly important. With the proliferation of different types of data and information available in today's world, no longer should decisions be made on "gut-feel" or a hunch. Breakthroughs in technology are enabling a more effective and efficient environment for business intelligence and analytics. Overall, there is a new generation of tools and capabilities to provide the right data to the right person at the right time!

1.5 Enabling a Competitive Advantage

As part of a large consulting firm, one of the authors helped to create a new Oracle BI practice. Centered around that practice was the concept of how corporations and organization could use analytics to gain a competitive advantage over their competitors. Numerous books now have been written of how some organizations—even from seemingly surprising industries such as baseball, namely, the Boston Red Sox—were using new BI tools for analysis that could help to beat their rivals. Utilizing analytics, these companies could measure and focus in on certain key indicators that would allow them to do such things as optimizing supply chains to identify their most profitable customers. Later that year, he wrote and published an article that recognized the trend toward operational BI and how it was rewriting the rules of competition, augmenting decisions and insights with facts, and slowly replacing the usual business practice of decision making with just instincts. With the maturity of BI systems and new technologies such as those involving Big Data to enable advanced analytics, a whole new level of business intelligence is possible.

BI and analytics are more than just a simple supply of data and information. BI solutions now encompass a holistic suite of capabilities that enables business strategy at all levels of decision making from tactical and operational to strategic to gain the competitive advantage. Organizations are now more capable of achieving high performance. High performing organizations have chosen to employ the distinctive capabilities of analytics to win over time and over their competitor. More and more companies have gained these capabilities, and the trend is toward an accelerated acceptance of analytics.

In their offerings, leading BI software vendor companies such as Oracle have pushed their message for organizations to gain a competitive advantage and become an "insight-driven enterprise." The plan entails the following:

1. Every person is provided with relevant, complete, and consistent information tailored to their function and role.
2. Intelligence provides insight that predicts the best next step, and delivers it in time to influence the business outcome.
3. Lead people take action based on facts to optimize decisions, actions, and interactions.

Sound simple enough, right? It's the same objective that has always been targeted. It seems that this may be easier said than done. From a practitioner's and implementer's point of view, we ask, "Why isn't everyone doing it successfully? What are the challenges?" Perhaps we don't have the right tools and technology to make it truly happen just yet. After all, even after a few decades into it, the field is still in its infancy. New capabilities are being discovered with every change and advancement in technology. Take, for instance, the concept for mobile BI. The idea is not at all new; however, in today's world of smartphones, mobile BI can now readily come to fruition. But not only that, other features and functions are just now being conceived and considered. With each new technological advance, BI will come closer to being able to offer organizations the means to transform into insight-driven enterprises.

But assuming that technology does get better and helps the BI industry overall, deep-rooted challenges still remain—especially when dealing with data. These issues are chronic, and we often hear stories of failed attempts at providing quality intelligence and analytics because of poor, inaccurate, or incomplete data. In fact even now, at the time of writing this book, there are other approaches and technologies (e.g., Big Data) being explored to effectively handle data. But our general perception is that it is not just about the technology. We don't dismiss the fact that fundamental shortcomings must first be fixed; however, other factors outside of technology come into play. These factors are related to understanding the various kinds of reporting and analytics being targeted and also knowing the data architecture and structures that support each kind of BI.

1.6 BI and Reporting Categories

Often, people will group tasks dealing with data or information as output under one heading as *Reporting*. In the simplest notion, reporting aims to provide access to data and information. Companies will often lump everything coming from the decision support system (DSS) and the output of transactional systems into one category, which they frequently call *reporting* or even sometimes *analytics*. But in this case, can "one size fit all" truly apply?

As a practitioner who must create and support such a system, you will discover that several considerations will come up that may easily form divisions in thought regarding the best methods to develop and handle that report. You begin to understand that different structures are involved with different types of reports. Furthermore, you begin to discover that what you are trying to achieve is not *Reporting* at all; rather, it is more of an *Analysis*. The end result is that you now know that there are different types of reporting. For our discussion concerning BI, reporting can be classified into three distinct categories:

- Operational Reporting
- Analytical BI
- Operational BI

Together, these three provide a holistic BI solution that covers all aspects of reporting and analysis. In the realm of BI, *Analytical BI* was the traditional form of BI, and it is often referred to as *Traditional BI*. With the industry now matured, what was once the traditional standard form of BI now has a place on its own and has made space for other forms of reporting and analytics. There are now other categories to complement Analytical BI: Operational Reporting and Operational BI, each having its own distinct purpose and goal, data source, and supporting data structure.

This book does not intend to go into detail as to how to implement each one but, for now, merely suggests that three different categories do exist. In recognizing this, you will achieve an understanding and gain knowledge of best practices for different types of online analytical processing (OLAP) solutions and, moreover, gain a vital understanding of what your own system or solution can offer and what its true capabilities are. Without that accurate, firsthand understanding of your systems and needs, incorrect solutions are often chosen, and as a result, expectations are not met. It is nearly impossible, in that case, to achieve the desired outcome and get what you want. We will focus on understanding how and where each form of reporting or analytics fits into the whole equation of providing a complete, holistic BI solution.

1.6.1 Operational Reporting

Operational Reporting is the type of reporting that is commonly performed; it is the one that is usually referred to when talking about reporting. Basically, this type of reporting is simply concerned with the current data from the online transactional processing (OLTP) system. An OLTP is an operational system which is used to capture business transactions and input data into the system.

This type of reporting usually comes in the form of a simple query of a certain entity within the system. For example, that query could ask "What is my customer list?" or "What is my product list?" The simple result and outcome would list these values. It does not concern itself with older or past data, mainly because the system may not contain that type of historical, trending data. This reporting can best be served and satisfied from the actual transactional system itself, as long as it contains reporting capabilities.

So take, for example, a customer with an enterprise resource planning (ERP) system installed and implemented. Most likely, that transactional system will inherently have a native mechanism for retrieving the data and producing a resulting output or report. In this case, no special architecture or redesign of the system is needed. In other words, a user should be able to request and produce a customer list simply by querying the customer entity in that application for a list of that data. In terms of quality, the operational system should ensure and handle the data input properly and subsequently store the data in the proper format so that it can be properly used later—including providing an accurate report of the data expected.

When retrieving a customer list, one would expect to find a field titled *first name* and another field titled *last name*. If so, then the system has properly formatted the data in the manner expected as an output. However, if this data is contained in a field that concatenates these two fields (first name and last name) along with some other information (such as Social Security number, for instance), then there would be a need to parse out that type of information to provide it in the expected format. The data would need to be restructured and reformatted beyond what is stored in the transactional system. With that said, though, it may not necessarily require an entirely new architecture and data structure to satisfy that request, as a complex analytical solution would entail.

1.6.2 Analytical BI

For an analytical solution or Analytical BI, an entirely different architecture and specialized data structure would be required to effectively handle that type of querying. That structure is referred to as a dimensional model or a star schema. Many books have been written on this subject matter, many of which are forwarded by Ralph Kimball, a pioneer in the data warehousing industry who championed that subject matter and provided practitioners with the crucial ingredient to building analytical solutions. As expert BI practitioners, we have come to understand and agree that the star schema and dimensional models are the appropriate architecture and structure for data warehouses and consequently BI solutions. Figure 1.1 shows how dimensions used in Analytical BI

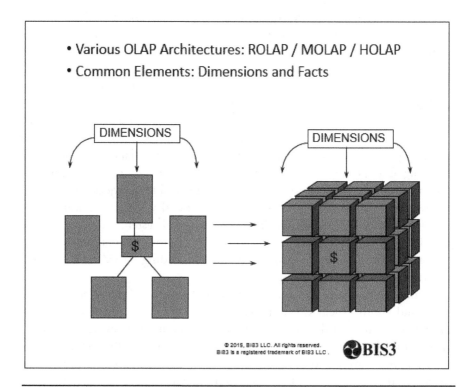

Figure 1.1 Dimensionality Exists Similarly in the Star Schema and Cube Used in Analytical BI. (Reproduced with permission from BIS3 LLC © 2015.)

exist similarly in various architectures, from a star schema in a relational database to a cube in a multidimensional structure.

As an overview, dimensional modeling serves to satisfy two major prongs when dealing with the development of an analytical solution. Those two prongs are: (1) user understandability and (2) performance. *User understandability* is when data is structured in such a way that a business user would understand it. It assumes that business users will analyze data by a metric or measurement that will form facts about a transaction. These facts are linked to and enriched by data in dimensions that are arranged in common identifiable business groupings.

A common example would be to look at the sale and the revenue of a company. The fact that is to be analyzed is "how much was sold." The dimensions most likely related to this metric of "how much was sold" are *by product*, *by employee*, and *by date*. In simple business terms, the organization might ask, "How much product was sold by a certain salesman in the second quarter of the year?" In technical terms, the query that would be formulated as: "Sum up the dollar amount that was sold by product, by employee, and by date." As stated earlier, the data would be stored dimensionally in a model containing the related information just described.

The second prong would have to deal with *performance* when querying the data stored in the database. For that, the star schema serves to offer an efficient structure for querying. If an analytical solution is desired, the data coming from the operational system must be redesigned and re-architected. This book does not intend to discuss how and why we think this structure is proper for a BI solution, but merely to say that, from experience and expertise, that this indeed is the proper structure and architecture required for effective BI solutions. In addition, this exercise of creating a dimensional model to structure the data is precisely what is going to prepare and subsequently populate a multidimensional structure or cube such as Essbase. This book, in later chapters, will provide some detail for using Essbase and will offer the reasons why it should be used and how it fits in today's landscape of BI tools, approaches to BI, and why it is to become Oracle's go-forward product for BI. Moreover, the book will discuss in detail how to create an analytical BI solution using a multidimensional cube.

In summary, we have discussed Operational Reporting and Analytical BI. We discussed how each approach has its own purpose and goal, how each comes from a different data source, and how each requires a specific type of data architecture and structure to best satisfy the request. Essentially, they exist in the opposite end of the spectrum—one comes from an OLTP system, the other from an OLAP system, as shown in Figure 1.2.

So it is simple if you have determined that you need one or the other—but what about requests that require some current data along with some historical data, with properties of both Operational Reporting and Analytical BI?

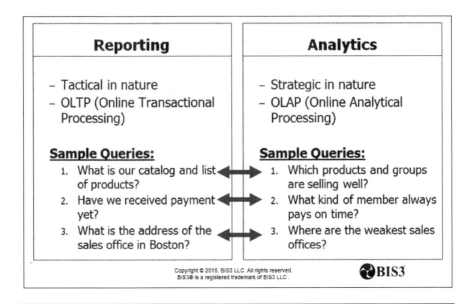

Figure 1.2   Reporting vs. Analytics—Examples in the Context of BI. (Reproduced with permission from BIS3 LLC © 2015.)

Furthermore, what if that type of reporting request cannot be effectively handled by either Operational Reporting structures or Analytical BI structures? Is there another type of reporting that exists that has properties of both Operational Reporting and Analytical BI, and is essentially a hybrid of both? Yes. That type of reporting is called Operational BI.

1.6.3 Operational BI

Operational BI entails transactional, up-to-date data displayed in the context of some sort of analysis. An example of this type of reporting could be "What products were sold to the top 10 customers of the month at the close of each business day?" This query cannot be answered solely by the operational system with its current list of customers, nor by the data warehouse storing the historical data from the prior day. Rather it depends on a certain combined analysis of the data coming from the integrated enterprise data warehouse supplying the list of the top 10 customers and the operational system providing the most current list of products sold during the day. Essentially, nowhere can this be provided except for a specially created structure called an *operational data store* that will contain current data along with some limited history provided.

Reporting + Analytics

- Tactical/Strategic
- ODS (Operational Data Store)

Sample Queries:

1. How many claims were processed before noon?
2. What is the total dues paid at this time?
3. How many policies did a particular salesperson close by COB?

 BIS3

Figure 1.3 Examples of Operational BI—Reporting *and* Analytics. (Reproduced with permission from BIS3 LLC © 2015.)

Figure 1.3 highlights examples of Operational BI involving both reporting and analytics.

It is important to discuss what type of structure would best satisfy that particular reporting request. In the history of BI, although analytics have served well when it comes to utilizing information of a historical nature, it still poses some problems and challenges when it comes to timing. In a traditional data warehouse, the timing to get data in to the warehouse is accomplished with an incremental nightly load. However, in the case of Operational BI, that may not be soon enough, and a mechanism may be required for loading data at or near real time.

So in technical terms, the basic conceptual difference and requirement needed for an Operational BI solution is that data has to be input into a structure that encompasses features from both an OLTP and OLAP structure combined, in which data integration is a major consideration along with the ability to perform efficiently for decision support. This structure is called an *operational data store*. It is essentially similar to the architecture of an enterprise data warehouse, but provides provision to satisfy an extra requirement in terms of more frequent loading and access to that data. Figure 1.4 depicts the typical solution architecture and data flow needed to support Operational BI.

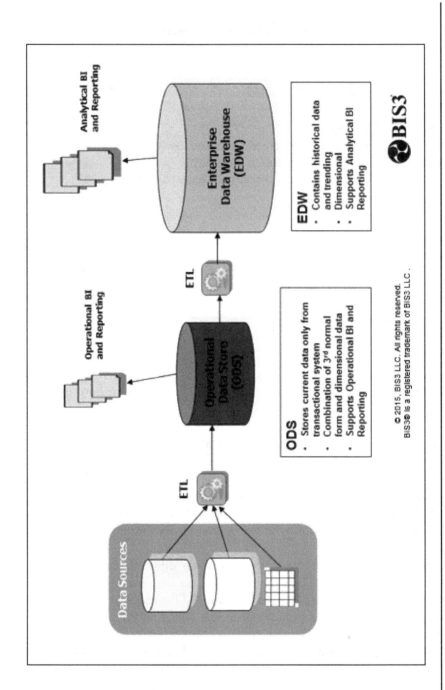

Figure 1.4 Typical Operational BI Architecture. (Reproduced with permission from BIS3 LLC © 2015.)

So in summary, there are various structures and architectures needed to satisfy certain data requests. If the request is for the most current data from a system, it can be accessed directly from the operational system itself; this is called Operational Reporting. On the other hand, if analysis of trending and historical data is the focus, then that request would be best satisfied by an enterprise data warehouse in the form of Analytical BI. This was the traditional form of BI, in which analysis of the most complete set of integrated data in a single repository is performed. As a hybrid of these two solutions, in the case where the requirement is to query current data along with some limited historical data provided at real or near-real time, this is most effectively achieved by leveraging a structure called an operational data store with Operational BI. These three categories for reporting and analytics—Operational Reporting, Analytical BI, and Operational BI—encompass all the reporting and analytical requirements and capabilities working together to utilize the data from the transactional system and make it readily available with a tool such as OBIEE.

1.7 Summary

This chapter outlined an introduction to a holistic BI solution in reference to the business context and relevance thereof. Starting with an emphasis on reporting, analysis, and analytics as a basic business need to drive decision making, it highlighted the need for BI and the various BI and reporting categories. It also outlined the use of Oracle Essbase and BI as components of such a holistic solution.

The next chapter examines the importance of Essbase and its relevance to modern-day multidimensional analysis and Analytical BI.

Chapter 2

Why Oracle Essbase Now

In This Chapter

2.1 Introduction

Oracle Business Intelligence Enterprise Edition (OBIEE)'s roots stem from Siebel Analytics. From a historical standpoint in the business intelligence (BI) industry, Siebel Analytics' prominence and rise came late in the game. At that time, other, more popular and visible BI tools were winning the market share in the nascent industry of BI in the late 1990s. Forward-thinking independent startup companies like Cognos and SAS were pushing the envelope for business intelligence. In those early days of the industry, there was a push to uncover all the possibilities of what BI and data warehousing (DW) could offer. As the industry took hold, many challenges were uncovered as the tools and the industry matured. It was clear that certain challenges had to be overcome in order to present BI as a capable, viable solution for doing analytics and providing the tools necessary for enabling decision support.

Those industry challenges can be summed up as:

- Visualizing data—how the information was presented
- Handling large volumes of data
- Distributing results and enterprise-wide access
- Effective data architecture and design
- Efficient movement of data from system to system
- Integrating data

Each one of these posed a major problem that needed to overcome in order to present a working holistic system and solution for BI and analytics. Some exist even today and have prompted the emergence of numerous technologies and approaches, such as Big Data and Big Data Analytics. Each of these new technologies and approaches boasts the same promise of overcoming the challenges that have historically plagued the industry.

2.2 OBIEE and Essbase: History and Importance

So what is the importance of discussing the history? Well, looking at the history provides an explanation and understanding of how the product was formulated, which in turn provides a good glimpse as to where the product will be heading. In other words, we will be able to gain knowledge and understand the true capabilities of an application and why it was developed as such. In the case of OBIEE, the application grew and was developed in an already mature market for what was then just a single specific extension of one specific application. It did not start out to become a premiere reporting and analytical solution. Almost by accident, it flourished into the powerful BI open platform that it is today.

It was indeed late in the game. However, because it developed in that manner, by the time that Siebel was acquired by Oracle, Siebel had gained some traction as a capable BI solution. Furthermore, because it was late in the game, they were able to recognize and strategize that integrating with certain popular, common systems at the time, such as Oracle EBS or PeopleSoft, would provide an advantage in offering prepackaged and preconfigured standard reports and dashboards that could easily be implemented in a much shorter time frame. In the midst of custom BI projects going over budget and over schedule, that proved to be quite a proposition and effective sales strategy. Essentially, it reduced the amount of time to develop and deliver the numerous BI and DW components that a standard BI solution would entail, as depicted in Figure 2.1.

If Siebel Analytics started off as a proprietary solution, it has certainly then evolved to not only provide a reporting mechanism and tool for its own Siebel transactional system but, more importantly, provided a true BI solution with

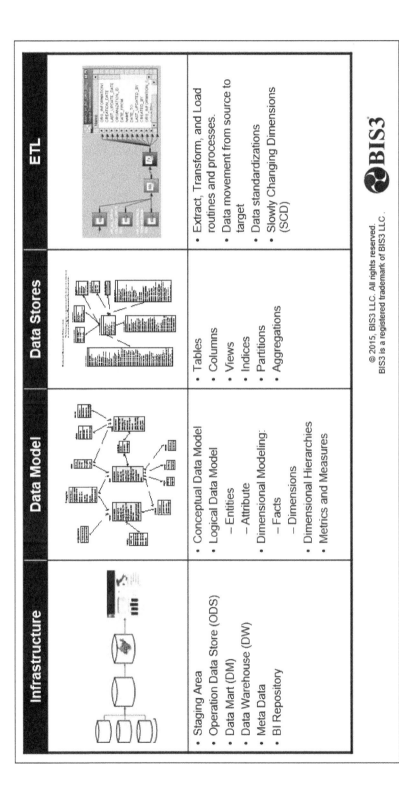

Infrastructure	Data Model	Data Stores	ETL

• Staging Area
• Operation Data Store (ODS)
• Data Mart (DM)
• Data Warehouse (DW)
• Meta Data
• BI Repository
	• Conceptual Data Model
	• Logical Data Model
	  – Entities
	  – Attribute
	• Dimensional Modeling:
	  – Facts
	  – Dimensions
	• Dimensional Hierarchies
	• Metrics and Measures
		• Tables
		• Columns
		• Views
		• Indices
		• Partitions
		• Aggregations
			• Extract, Transform, and Load routines and processes.
			• Data movement from source to target
			• Data standardizations
			• Slowly Changing Dimensions (SCD)

BIS3

Figure 2.1 BI under the Covers. (Reproduced with permission from BIS3 LLC © 2015.)

an open architecture that enabled it to source data from any system. Moreover, because it gained prominence at a later stage in a relatively mature market, it was developed and encompassed what was, at the time, established tried and true best practices of BI. These best practices included:

- Utilizing the star schema architecture
- Using a best-of-breed extract, transform, and load (ETL) tool (embedded into the solution)
- Providing a browser-based front-end

These were included as a standard part of the solution offering and helped catapult the product forward, despite the fact that it was "late to the party." However, being a latecomer may have actually greatly contributed to the product's success. For instance, while others were arguing about which architecture would best support the querying and decision support systems used for analytics, the Siebel Analytics product had already incorporated dimensional models and the star schema architecture from the beginning. Essentially, what this meant was that the solution offering already had a solid base for development, having incorporated proven best practices. So when Oracle acquired Siebel, Oracle also acquired a much-needed and more effective BI product to replace its existing BI product at that time.

Since acquiring Siebel and the Siebel Analytics product, now repackaged as OBIEE, Oracle has been able to gather its BI strategy cohesively and create a new standard and offering for its own product. It can be said that the acquisition provided a movement toward fulfilling what Oracle's customers were looking for all along: a mechanism for being able to report from its operational system (i.e., Oracle EBS) seamlessly and effectively.

Oracle has retired—or is planning to retire—its old products and is now moving toward having an established reporting tool. The company is on the verge of adding to its established reporting and analytics platform by adding capabilities for other BI functions and mechanisms for data discovery, ETL, and cubes for Analytical BI. The last of these has been satisfied by the incorporation of a multidimensional analytical server called Essbase. This book explores why Essbase is now being added as the foundation and what is prompting this need.

Keep in mind that traditional BI offerings included a multidimensional structure or cube as a standard component. OBIEE, or the former Siebel Analytics, was a relational online analytical processing (ROLAP) solution, and not a MOLAP solution using a multidimensional structure. With the use of Essbase, a more traditional approach to BI, or what is now referred to as Analytical BI, is now possible.

2.3 Why Essbase Now: From History to Historical, Analytical, and Beyond

From its humble beginnings as a product of Arbor Software in 1992 (when it introduced the first version of Essbase) to becoming part of Hyperion Solutions in 1998, Essbase has been growing in functionality as multidimensional OLAP (MOLAP) software. Oracle acquired Hyperion in 2007 and integrated Hyperion's BI tools into OBIEE Plus. As of 2009, Essbase had been commercialized as an Oracle product, as Oracle Essbase, and had been introduced as part of Oracle's BI Suite. A history of Essbase can be obtained from the in2Hyperion website (http://www.in2hyperion.com/page/Hyperion-Essbase.aspx), and an in-depth overview of Oracle Essbase can be found on Oracle's website (http://www.oracle.com/us/solutions/business-analytics/business-intelligence/essbase/overview/index.html).

Here are a few reasons why Oracle Essbase matters now more than ever:

- As enterprises shifted toward integrated IT environments with heterogeneous systems, OLAP anaylsis involved more than querying the Oracle Database. Oracle Essbase, with its capability to address heterogeneous source systems, became a trend setter for multidimensional analysis.
- From the late 1990s to today, the number of concurrent users rapidly grew from less than a hundred to thousands. The same explosive growth is true for data. This increase necessitated OLAP analysis to support this growth; Oracle Essbase, with its enriched functionality, is better suited for this.
- Oracle Essbase, as part of Hyperion acquisition, can power EPM solutions based on Hyperion. This is critical to today's business needs, as it enables the measurement of the key performance indicators involved, which in turn drives business decisions.
- It also allows what-if analysis and scenario modeling—the basis for using Essbase to address predictive analytics.
- Essbase has a uniquely business-centric implementation, rather than being focused on database administration.
- Oracle Essbase is consumer-focused and independent of the Database. It has complete multidimensional functionality, capable of addressing modern-day and next-gen OLAP analysis.
- As a result of the gap of OBIEE's inability to fully address predictive analytics, Oracle Essbase enables cube-based predictive analytics using the analytical power of cubes and MDX structures. This is where Oracle Essbase can be utilized for analytical BI and its future as a next-generation OLAP server.
- OLAP analysis became more in-depth, requiring complete highly complex multidimensional analysis involving MDX, XML/A OLAP-aware

querying and planning, forecasting, and allocations. Oracle's OLAP-based SQL OLAP was not quite suitable for addressing these needs.

• Essbase is now fully embedded and integrated into OBIEE.

Essbase has always been a dominant player and leader in multidimensional or cube technologies. Its developers' use of cutting-edge technology and forward thinking have paved the way for the development and evolution of business intelligence and its capabilities. Coupled with definitive business metrics and goals, Essbase has become a formidable tool for decision making and analytics for business users. However, it is more than just a tool; its technology and capabilities for handling and summarizing large amount of data dynamically recommend it as a critical component of the total strategy for a good BI package and solution. In this case, Essbase provides aggregations and summaries as part of a holistic and comprehensive BI solution with cubes—something that was lacking in the earlier versions of OBIEE and the former Siebel Analytics.

Through its acquisition and evolution with Oracle, the plan for Essbase was always to become fully embedded as an integral part of the Oracle Business Intelligence Suite—and now that has come to pass. Although it still exists and can be used as a standalone product, it is now a component (i.e., Essbase Business Intelligence Accelerator Wizard) used in conjunction with the RPD of OBIEE for an aggregation strategy to essentially speed up reporting and analysis. Now more than ever, as it heavily relies on the logical data model (via the RPD) with a common and "single version of the truth," it has become a vital part of the holistic, comprehensive solution for business intelligence and analytics for the Oracle Business Intelligence Suite.

Throughout this book, the authors have emphasized the creation of a logical (dimensional) data model as a blueprint for multidimensional analysis and extension and customization of Essbase for analytical BI and beyond. This still holds true for current users with Essbase installations as a standalone tool and also now especially for new users with installations of the integrated Essbase and OBIEE package.

2.4 Summary

This chapter examined the important role of Essbase and how it evolved in modern multidimensional analysis and in the BI solution landscape. Starting with a history of BI and its role in business decision making, the chapter highlighted why it matters now more than ever to use Essbase as a component of a holistic BI solution. The next chapter will highlight the successful players and products of Oracle Essbase and BI.

Chapter 3

Oracle Essbase and Oracle BI: Successful Players and Products

In This Chapter

3.1 Introduction

The technology that supports using Oracle Essbase and Oracle BI for comprehensive business intelligence (BI) starts with implementing Oracle Essbase as an online analytical processing (OLAP) solution through data integration, then using it for Analytical BI. Oracle Essbase provides forward-facing analysis via its ability to model what-if scenarios and forecast future trends. It goes a step further by providing end user–enabled custom analytics, which can be augmented by Oracle BI and Oracle BI Enterprise Edition (OBIEE) for operational and interactive BI. While discussing the successful players and products, it is imperative to list the same categorized under multiple areas of OLAP and BI space. These include engineered solutions, enterprise reporting, OLAP Analytics, Enterprise BI, self-service, operational, interactive, mobile BI, and most recently Big Data. Oracle BI provides the ease of deployment on the platform of choice that includes on-premise, on-cloud, or on-mobile.

Together, Oracle Essbase and Oracle BI provide a practical solution that stands out as an example of end-to-end BI that incorporates interactive visualizations and dynamic dashboarding; in-memory, mobile, data discovery, Big Data, and predictive analytics; and across-the-business dimensions of analytical and operational analysis and decision making—while at the same time providing performance visibility and a user-friendly experience. It also provides insight into using self-service and advanced analytics to solve business problems. And it plugs seamlessly into existing infrastructure.

3.2 The Primary Vendors: Inventors and Presenters

The primary vendors include Siebel and Hyperion, which have now acquired by Oracle. These are the inventors. In addition to this, vendors of other relational databases and SAP Business Warehouse (BW) can be presenters of OLAP analysis by using Oracle Essbase as a stand-alone OLAP server for the purposes of analytical reporting and trend analysis. The presenters deserve special mention, as stated in the following:

- Oracle Essbase and Oracle Essbase Studio, along with financial reporting tools primarily for what-if analysis
- Oracle BI Foundation Suite that can be used to integrate Oracle Essbase and OBIEE providing a complete BI solution
- Oracle Fusion Middleware, which is an enclosing product for Oracle Essbase
- Oracle Fusion Applications
- Siebel Analytics, on which OBIEE is based, acquired by Oracle in 2005
- Oracle Endeca Information Discovery software acquired by Oracle in late 2011—tailored for unstructured analysis, self-service information discovery
- Oracle Hyperion Smart View for Office for integrating OBIEE with Microsoft Office

- Oracle BI seamlessly integrates with Oracle E-Business Suite, PeopleSoft Enterprise, JD Edwards Enterprise One, Hyperion Planning, Oracle Application Express (APEX), Oracle Endeca Information Discovery, and Oracle BI Discoverer

The inventors and presenters, along with their products, expand Oracle BI and extend analytics beyond traditional reporting and key performance indicators (KPIs) to support advanced analytics, including prescriptive and predictive analytics. This in turn provides access to the same, more pervasively (i.e., to a wider range of users), while at the same time making it more business user–driven, resulting in scale-out BI.

3.3 The Primary Products and Tools Set: Inclusions and Exclusions

3.3.1 Oracle Exalytics

Oracle Exalytics is an in-memory system engineered to run Oracle BI and Enterprise Performance Management (EPM) products. It comes embedded with OBIEE 11g and Oracle Essbase (ASO and BSO), along with TimesTen in-memory cache. It leverages in-memory optimized hardware, in-memory Oracle BI, Essbase, TimesTen, and Endeca to provide relational, fully multidimensional, unstructured analytics, analytical reporting, and financial and operational planning. The inherent Oracle BI Foundation Suite provides extreme performance for relational OLAP (ROLAP) and multidimensional OLAP (MOLAP) analysis involving Big Data scale and enterprise-wide performance management applications. It also delivers advanced data visualization capabilities that enable granular visual exploration. The following points deserve special mention with regard to Oracle Exalytics and improved Oracle BI and Essbase performance:

- Oracle Exalytics enables the caching of OBIEE metadata models and the data from Essbase cubes into memory. This ensures performance at the BI application level.
- Oracle Essbase cubes can be easily deployed to run on Oracle Exalytics, resulting in a seamless integration that yields n times faster performance and scalability. OBIEE deployed in Oracle Exalytics is easier to maintain than that deployed on commodity hardware.
- Oracle Exalytics Summary Advisor, which is also in-memory and self-optimizing, gathers usage statistics on queries to determine which data is to be loaded into memory versus left on disk.

- Oracle Exalytics' in-memory performance architecture enables interactive dashboard analyses of multimillion-row sets—analyses that are forward-looking; the datasets involved are larger in terms of velocity and variety.
- Oracle Exalytics can be integrated with Oracle Exadata via a fast Infiniband connection, opening the door for direct access to enterprise data warehouses and seamless data flow from Oracle Exadata to Exalytics.
- Oracle Exalytics is more integrated into Oracle's product stack with less support for multiple BI vendors.

Nucleus Research's Research Note: "Examining The Value Of Oracle Exalytics" provides insight into the business value of Oracle Exalytics' greater visibility, increased productivity and efficiency, scalability, and lower total cost of ownership (TCO). It is available at http://www.oracle.com/us/solutions/ent-performance-bi/business-intelligence/examining-value-oracle-exalytics-1976483.pdf.

3.3.2 Oracle Essbase

Oracle Essbase is a standalone OLAP server owned and controlled by Oracle as part of its Hyperion acquisition. It is a fully functional OLAP server external to the Oracle database that is part of the Common Enterprise Information Model and under the umbrella of Oracle Fusion Middleware. It provides MDX and XML/A as opposed to SQL Access, thus enabling full multidimensional access to OLAP data. It is end user–centric and can be used across heterogeneous environments. Its potential lies in its ability to function as an OLAP engine for Hyperion performance management solutions and forecasting and planning tools. The uniqueness of Essbase lies in its business-centric implementation rather than database administration. It also supports write-back capabilities to its multidimensional cubes. The following features make Oracle Essbase a key choice for OLAP Analytics in conjunction with Oracle Database and OBIEE:

- Connectivity to multisource heterogeneous relational databases via open database connectivity (ODBC), including SAP BW
- MDX query language, the standard for OLAP querying—cubes accessed using MDX and XML/A (for Web Analysis)
- Analytic Integration Services, Administration Services, Provider Services, and Hyperion Shared Services
- Java, MDX and XML/A API and Smart View-based communication
- Hybrid Analysis
- Integration with BI Publisher, financial and interactive reporting, and Web Analysis

- Search functionality
- Workspace and Excel Add-in

3.3.3 Oracle BI Publisher

Oracle BI Publisher is a common platform for creating and delivering for operational reporting over the Web or using familiar desktop tools such as Microsoft Word and Adobe Acrobat. Oracle BI Publisher allows separation of the data query from the report template, thus enabling a single query to be associated with multiple report templates at runtime. This allows for report bursting tailored towards multiple users with customized content. Oracle BI Publisher can be deployed as a stand-alone or as part of OBIEE. The following points highlight some features and functionality about BI Publisher:

- It supports heterogeneous data sources, including Web Services, XML-based sources, and external files. It also supports connections to Oracle Endeca data stores. Using Endeca Query Language (EQL) queries, data can be selected from Oracle Endeca Server and used in BI Publisher reports.
- It supports a variety of output formats, such as PDF for pixel-perfect reporting, HTML for reports over the Web, and CSV and XML for exporting to external systems. The interactive report mode and multiple report templates are optimized for high performance delivery of all output formats.
- It supports reports that can print in multiple languages.
- It is hot-pluggable and be seamlessly integrated with custom applications using Web services or Java API.
- It is end user–oriented, enabling the creation of report layouts by dragging-and-dropping custom business indicators using BI Publisher's layout editor. The integration of OBIEE dashboards with BI Publisher layout editor enables PDF generation of the dashboard that can be imported into BI Publisher to autogenerate a printable format.
- It enables scheduling of custom report jobs based on a trigger. A retry limit can be set to auto-re-execute that trigger on its failure.

3.3.4 Oracle BI Foundation Suite

Oracle BI Foundation Suite, also termed Oracle BI Foundation, provides an integrated platform for operational reporting, dashboards, ad hoc query and analysis using ROLAP, MOLAP, planning and budgeting, unstructured analytics, and predictive analytics. Also, users can leverage all of this on the mobile platform of their choice ensuring data quality and security. It enables metadata to be shared consistently across OLTP sources, ODS, data warehouse, data marts, Essbase cubes, and Apache Hadoop data sources resulting in federated views of data.

It includes features such as visualizations and interactions, office and smart view functionality, BI Mobile HD, BI Publisher, and BI Server for Big Data and Exalytics. Oracle BI Foundation Suite also includes OBIEE with dashboard analytics and common enterprise semantic model as its components. The latest release supports the following enhancements:

- Visualizations and user interactivity
  - Data-driven visualizations driven by recommendation views that enable selection based on content and context of the analysis. It also gives the flexibility of how data can be controlled using multiple views in the same analysis.
  - Performance tiles that display a set of metrics on a dashboard that are user-customizable.
  - New visualizations such as waterfall graphs, map views, 100% stacked charts, breadcrumbs, and trellis view actions in a dashboard all enhance user interaction experience. Freeze columns for tables, pivots, and advanced trellis views anchor the headers at the top of the view even as the user scrolls down the dataset. Freeze columns are also available in Oracle BI Mobile through the Oracle BI Mobile HD app via a two-finger swipe gesture.
  - Integrated search functionality via the Endeca Information Discovery server gives the end user/business analyst the power to do a full-text search based on attribute filters like *type*, *name*, *created by*, and so on.
- Oracle Mobile BI HD
  Mobile-friendly gestures such as double-tapping and touch-screen interactions enable better interaction in leveraging the improvements to visualizations. Also users can take advantage of Oracle BI Publisher mobile improvements to open and view BI Publisher reports and locally save them for offline consumption. Additionally, the Oracle BI Mobile Security Toolkit included in the latest version of Oracle BI Foundation Suite provides a repackaged, unsigned, and uncertified version of Oracle BI Mobile HD app that allows a customizable way to integrate third-party mobile device management (MDM) security solution, sign it with its corporate signature, and deploy it on the chosen delivery platform.

- Integration with Hadoop
  Oracle BI Foundation Suite 11g supports integration with Hadoop data sources via a Hive ODBC interface. Using direct commands from Oracle BI Server to Hive, querying and fetching data from Hadoop sources is possible.
- Oracle Essbase integration
  The seamless integration of Oracle BI Foundation Suite with Oracle Essbase provides write-back to Essbase cubes from OBIEE and Essbase as an Aggregate Persistence target.
- Other enhancements
  - It supports the export of dashboards to BI Publisher. BI Publisher reports are automatically rendered in the background. Additionally, dashboard content can also be exported to Microsoft Office formats—Excel and PowerPoint. Also, template-based printing of dashboards is supported.
  - It offers users the flexibility to create subject area reports that run directly against the Oracle BI Server. This eliminates the need to create an extra BI Publisher data model.
  - It supports Smart View integration with Office via the Oracle Hyperion Smart View for Office. The BI Presentation Catalog in Smart View enables secure BI dashboard page and report prompts using single sign-on, and BI View creation in Smart View allows creation of Answers views from Excel.

3.3.5 Oracle BI Enterprise Edition (OBIEE)

OBIEE is a powerful and comprehensive business intelligence and analytics platform. It includes interactive dashboards, ad-hoc, published and operational reporting including financial reporting, integrated analytics on any data-set, any data source and in any format; unstructured, predictive and mobile analytics, proactive notifications and alerts, actionable intelligence, Microsoft Office integration, scorecards, and server based query, analysis and reporting. OBIEE is part of Oracle Fusion Middleware and is embedded in Oracle Fusion Applications. On the same lines Oracle BI Standard Edition One provides the same enterprise-class functionality to small and medium businesses that helps them in making better business decisions.

OBIEE incorporates a common enterprise semantic model through its repository—what is commonly referred to as the RPD. The RPD is an enterprise metadata layer that encompasses all data sources—from Big Data (Apache Hadoop) to in-memory sources like Oracle TimesTen to OLAP sources like

Essbase, flat files, XML, Web Services, relational database management system (RDBMSs) and third-party sources. OBIEE can seamlessly integrate with Essbase for reporting data. The OBIEE logical model can be used as a data source for Essbase. *It is also possible to write-back to Essbase cubes from OBIEE.*

Taking OBIEE as an example of a BI solution that addresses multiple facets of business needs, the following list gives a glimpse into the capabilities such a solution can provide:

- Near real-time and right-time reporting on operational data
- Business analysis across multiple dimensions using MOLAP
- Analysis and reporting on historical data using ROLAP
- Comparative analysis with financial planning, budgeting, and forecasting data
- Predictive analytics to determine future outcomes using statistical models and other forms of predictive models
- Analysis of Big Data, including machine-generated data, to identify patterns and correlations (Please refer to the article in Ref. 1 for a generic outline of using the cloud to unleash the potential of Big Data.)[1]

OBIEE 11g enables greater dashboard interactivity for the end user and improved data visualization over its previous versions. Of primary mention are the following:

- Oracle Summary Advisor, which can help improve performance
- Oracle BI Composer, a user-friendly wizard for creating analyses
- OBIEE's new visual discovery functionality when deployed with Oracle Exalytics
- Contextual suggestions, recommending the best-fit visualization type vis-à-vis current data
- Performance tiles, which provide instant summary metrics
- Compare and contrast data distributions using stacked bars
- Correlation between initial values and series of intermediate values using waterfall charts
- Comparative analysis by way of display of data-dense views in the form of trellis chart grids
- Contextual navigation actions and awareness
- Full-text search using Endeca MDEX technology that is context based, augmented by visual analytics; Oracle Endeca supports self-service data discovery, considered as a component of mainstream BI
- *Save As* option for dashboard analysis
- Export of dashboards and dashboard content to native Excel and PowerPoint formats

- Smart Views that serves as the primary Office application that encloses BI presentation catalogs and allows BI view creation, a feature that enables BI answers view creation directly in Excel, and saving the same to Excel
- Export of dashboard to BI Publisher, with autocreation of the data model and report based on it
- Pixel-perfect printing of dashboards; also, attachment of multiple templates to the dashboard and the preservation of dashboard state

OBIEE 11g excels in its support for Big Data analytics, which include native integration with Hive, Hadoop MapReduce, and HDFS. The Oracle BI Server uses auto-generated HiveQL/ODBC to query data directly from Hadoop. It can also be used to interface with Oracle Exalytics for integrated analysis of Big Data and real-time streaming/social media data.

Last but not the least, OBIEE supports self-service BI capabilities and actionable intelligence by way of its dynamic dashboarding, user-interactivity enhancements, and proactive detection and alerting. Oracle BI also supports process intelligence. The OBIEE Action Framework enables invocation of business processes from within dashboards and reports, querying of business activity monitoring data, and analysis of the same. This boils down to turning insight into actions. This ability can be further enhanced to accelerate self-service BI by way of a feedback loop into the BI application in context that incorporates the same as BI rules to improvise and autogenerate better decisions using the BI dashboard.

3.3.6 Oracle BI Mobile

Oracle BI Mobile is a leading platform that provides greater BI outreach to growing number of users and enables the development of customized code-free applications tailored toward business needs. The Mobile BI platform supports apps for both smart phones and tablets that are interactive and business user–focused. Oracle BI Mobile architecture enables development, deployment, and maintenance of mobile apps across a variety of devices while at the same time ensuring the security of critical data and master data management involved. It uses the same security model as Oracle BI, thereby eliminating the need to separately build security for the business users. This strategy provides for BI anywhere, anytime, and by anyone authorized. It also allows offline viewing and sharing of BI content and online synchronization of saved offline content. Also the mobile apps can be monitored for its usage and patterns using the integrated Oracle Fusion Middleware Audit Framework. Oracle Mobile BI Platform includes:

- Oracle Mobile BI HD
  This Mobile BI app for smartphones and tablets enables seamless deployment of new or existing analytic content such as interactive dashboards, scorecards, and reports. It is integrated with Oracle BI Foundation Suite, supports location intelligence, and provides build-once, consume-anywhere access across the enterprise without any rework.
- Oracle Mobile BI App Designer
  This allows the business user to easily develop do-it-yourself analytic mobile applications that are purpose-built toward a line of business. It does this by way of a web browser–based drag-and-drop interface that is codeless and autorendering for variable screen sizes using its adaptive Web engine. Fully integrated with Oracle BI Foundation Suite, it allows data from existing BI environments to be consumed for actionable BI.

  The apps run using HTML5 on iOS, Android, Windows Mobile, and BlackBerry devices. The final output can be previewed using a browser based mobile simulator or by scanning QR code that is autogenerated by the BI App Designer.

  It is touch enabled for easy browsing through the data in context, and the interactive visualizations allow for drill-anywhere functionality on any dataset, to provide key insights for improved decision making. The toolbar menu and navigation pages ease the task of directly finding the data on which users need to base their analyses. Users can also create an App Library for sharing apps tailored towards a particular line of business.

3.3.7 Oracle BI Applications

Oracle BI Applications are a set of prebuilt BI solutions that enable businesses to buy and extend their BI implementations and at the same time deliver timely insight anywhere and anytime. It is built on a 100 percent open platform and incorporates industry-standard metrics, giving users the capability to define their own metrics on top of the packaged functional content. Its state-of-the-art analytics coupled with next-generation BI foundation enable faster, better, and deep-dive fact-based analysis. Leveraging the power of Enterprise Oracle Data Integrator (ODI), it includes a comprehensive integration platform that gives direct access to federated data sources. It also enables extract, transform, and load (ETL) validation and allows the tracking of data lineage from source to target, thereby providing data transparency across the business. Also, Oracle BI Applications run on Exalytics. The following are the primary applications included in the latest release 11.1.1.7.1 of Oracle BI Applications solutions, encompassing horizontal and vertical domains:

- Student Information Analytics
- Indirect Spend Planning
- ERP Analytics
  - Financial Analytics
  - HR Analytics
  - Project Analytics
  - Procurement and Spend Analytics
  - Supply Chain and Order Management Analytics
- Customer Relationship Management (CRM) Analytics
  - Sales
  - Marketing
  - Service
  - Contact Center
  - Price
  - Loyalty
- Enterprise Performance Management (EPM) Applications
  - Strategic Planning
  - Financial Close
  - Planning and Forecasting
  - Profitability Management
- Industry Analytics
  - Healthcare
  - Communications
  - Retail
  - Public Sector
  - Financial Services
- New tools to accelerate Oracle BI Applications that include Data Lineage Analysis, ETL Validation Utility, Configuration Manager, and Functional Setup Manager
- Oracle Data Integrator Integration using in-database extract, load, transform (E-LT) transformation and declarative design
- Oracle Golden Gate Integration

3.3.8 Oracle BI for Big Data

The Big Data scenario demands optimizing BI environments for meeting the analysis of increased volumes, variety, and velocity data. Oracle BI for BI Data addresses these requirements by providing:

- In-memory analytics and BI

- Integration of Big Data and decision making
- Advanced data visualization
- Enhanced interactivity
- Faster dashboards
- Expanded and high-performance analytics
- Better performance
- Better administration tools for lower TCO

Oracle BI Server provides Hadoop integration and complex event processing (CEP) integration. Oracle Exalytics can be leveraged against Big Data and continuous data sources. Additionally, Oracle Big Data Appliance is an engineered system that is specifically designed for delivering real-time insight to action by way of instant analyses of Big Data. It includes Hadoop, NoSQL, and very large dataset support. Oracle Endeca Information Discovery can be used for self-service data discovery on structured and unstructured data, thereby enabling data-driven decisions on the variety of data.

3.4 The Primary Users: Evaluators, Investors, Implementers and Eventual Benefiters

With primary focus on the metrics by way of advanced analytics, a complete BI solution can go a long way in setting the standard for best practice metrics. This delivers faster time to value and a superior customer experience. It gives a big boost for businesses that are investing in and implementing such solutions and opens up a strategy of build versus buy and extend for customers hoping to leverage existing deployments.

An Oracle Essbase and OBIEE solution designed on the key factors of in-memory analytics, data discovery, mobile, Big Data, cloud, and predictive analytics becomes the solution of choice for business analysts, IT executives, and customers alike.

Customers investing in and implementing Oracle BI Foundation Suite and the BI platform gain the benefits of:

- Faster and better analysis on large datasets that includes any data from any data source and in any format.
- Improved BI performance and scalability that ranges from department level to enterprise wide, in addition to rich functionality, information access, and seamless integration with the rest of BI stack.

- Prebuilt and industry-tailored packaged analytic applications that are integrated contextually and can be deployed on premise, on cloud, or on mobile. BI in the cloud enables scale-out BI across increased user base and multitenant workloads.
- Oracle BI Solution-in-a-Box investors derive the benefit of enterprise class BI deployment at a lower TCO and higher return on investment (ROI). As described on the Oracle website (http://www.oracle.com/bi), Oracle BI Solution-in-a-Box includes the Oracle database with partitioning, diagnostics, and tuning, Oracle BI Foundation Suite, and ODI, all running in two Oracle virtual machines on the Oracle Database Appliance.

From a technical standpoint:

- OBIEE is an implementer of Oracle Essbase to report against its data (i.e., use Essbase as a data source for OBIEE and vice versa).
- OBIEE and BI stack benefit from Oracle Essbase, in that the latter can add performance and analytic functionality to both.

Business analysts and end users can significantly benefit from:

- Using OBIEE-enhanced and extensible visualizations and user-interaction functionality, Microsoft Office integration features, and Mobile BI improvements
- Using Oracle Endeca Information Discovery for self-service search-based BI
- Using Oracle BI Applications (OBIA) to leverage industry-specific and standards-based integrated analytics solutions deployable with existing Oracle BI infrastructure

System implementers can align business requirements with the appropriate Oracle BI tools set to create a perfect implementation scenario—especially in case of buy and extend.

Implementation specialists can benefit from:

- Using ODI and Oracle Golden Gate to eliminate data integration challenges, thereby easing the integration between OBIA and the BI platform
- Using OBIA's new tools to accelerate the deployment of the same, such as Configuration Manager, Functional Setup Manager, Data Lineage Analysis, and ETL Validation Utility

BI developers can benefit from:

- All of the new and enhanced visualizations and dynamic dashboarding functionality in delivering BI content that provides extensibility and ease of self-service to the end user

- Oracle BI Mobile advancements in providing the BI Mobile consumer with anytime, anywhere, any-device access to information and delivery of the same
- OBIEE functionality for pervasive integration between Oracle Essbase and OBIEE for broader access of Essbase data to end users
- Essbase and OBIEE security alignment
- Write-back feature to Essbase cube from OBIEE
- And last but not the least, getting to know how the user base is leveraging Oracle BI tools

---

Gartner's 2014 Magic Quadrant for Business Intelligence and Analytics Platforms describes Oracle's BI platform positioned as follows with regard to its customer base:

> *Customers choose Oracle for its integration within solutions based on Oracle applications and technology. In particular, Oracle offers over 80 prebuilt analytic applications for Oracle E-Business Suite, People-Soft, JD Edwards, Siebel and other enterprise applications, including industry-specific packaged analytic applications. These analytic applications include prebuilt ETL, data warehouse models, KPIs, reports and dashboards. Oracle BI analytics optimizations with Oracle Essbase and the Oracle Hyperion Enterprise Performance Management platform enable customers to implement an end-to-end analytic process for financial budgeting, planning, consolidation, and close processes. Oracle also has integration between Oracle BI, Oracle Complex Event Processing and Oracle Real-Time Decisions to support real-time event detection and analysis. However, the complexity of analysis conducted by Oracle customers who responded to our survey is less than that indicated by customers of most of the other vendors in the survey. (Source: https://www.gartner.com/doc/2668318/ magic-quadrant-business-intelligence-analytics)*

By way of extending analysis, Oracle Essbase and OBIEE thus make all relevant data accessible to decision makers. Leveraging a combination of its analytics and tools set, OBIA, Oracle BI and Oracle Mobile BI allows BI users and analysts to transform their organizations in an analysis-centric, user-friendly and IT-compliant manner. This can be applied at all levels of the organization starting from the department level to the enterprise level in the following manner:

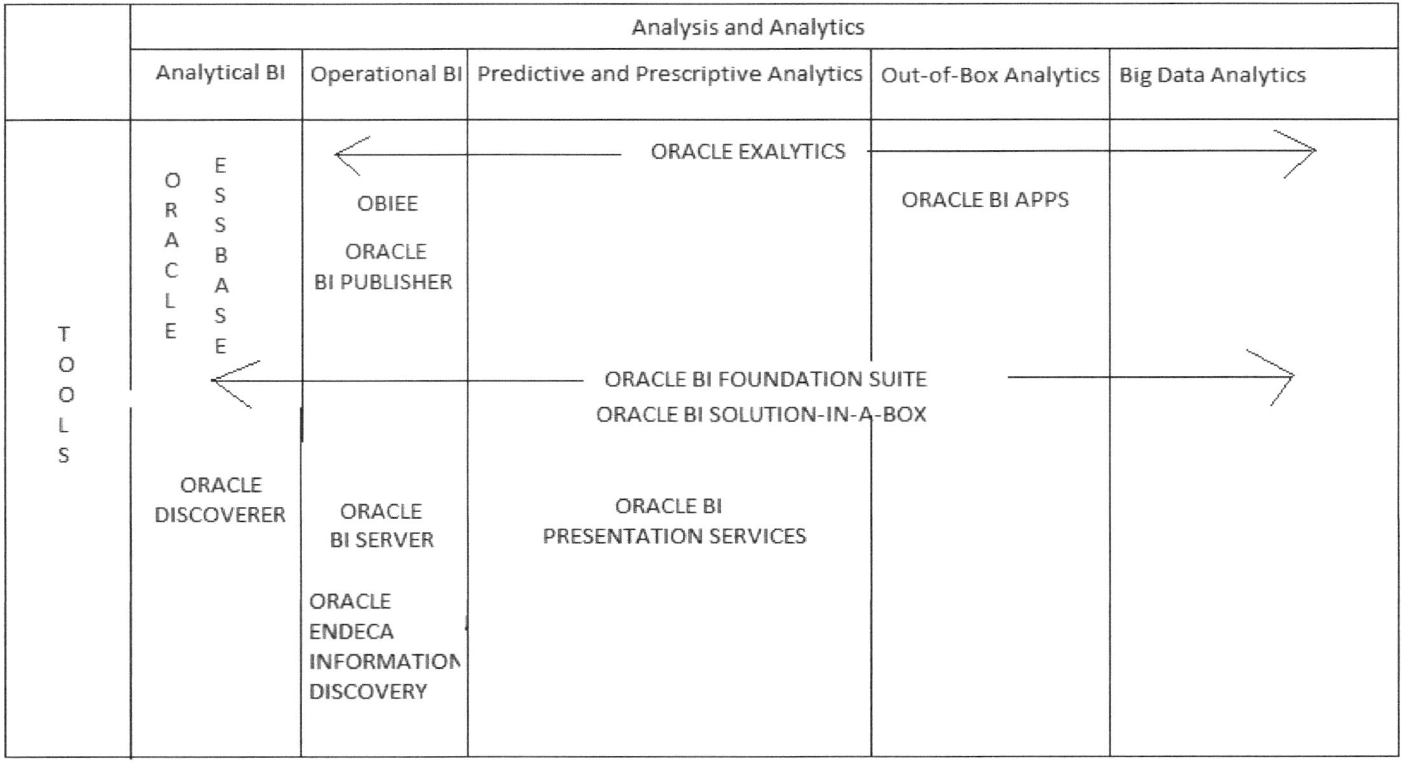

Figure 3.1 High-Level View of Oracle Essbase and BI Tools versus Analysis and Analytics Operations

(See description of Figure 3.1 on page 36.)

- Sourcing internal and external data in a federated manner, thereby providing direct access to source data
- Deriving analytics that power performance using Oracle BI Server
- Delivering analysis dashboards and scorecards that combine descriptive and predictive analytics using Oracle BI Presentation Services
- Going a step further in using optimization techniques to provide proactive BI solutions that deliver prescriptive analytics

Figure 3.1 gives a high-level view of Oracle Essbase and BI tools versus analysis and analytics operations.

3.5 Summary

This chapter dealt with the successful players and products of Oracle Essbase and OBIEE in terms of the primary vendors, products and tools set, and primary users. It highlighted the features and functionality in Oracle's product suite and how each one fits into the larger landscape of analytical, operational, and mobile BI. The next chapter focuses on the analysis, evaluation, and selection of Oracle Essbase and Oracle BI as a comprehensive BI solution with emphasis on essential criteria, critical deciding factors, and the final pick as a customer-centric solution.

3.6 References

1. Lakshman Bulusu, "Using the Cloud to Unleash the Potential of Big Data." Presentation: Data Summit 2014, May 12–14, 2014, New York, NY; http://www.dbta.com/DataSummit/2014/presentations.aspx.

Chapter 4

Analysis, Evaluation, and Selection

In This Chapter

4.1 Introduction

Building a real-world application using Oracle Essbase and Oracle Business Intelligence Enterprise Edition (OBIEE) requires strategic planning and analysis of the business processes involved and how well they can be implemented in such a solution from design to dashboard and beyond. The essential criteria can be broadly classified into the following categories:

- Business process discovery
- Information integration
- Information dissemination

- Information transformation
- Information visualization
- User interaction
- Information customization
- Information in action: BI, advanced analytics, and beyond BI (competitive, social, and cloud-based intelligence)
- Information and Big Data

This chapter will examine each of the above categories based on how best Oracle Essbase and OBIEE can together be used to achieve implementation of the same to improve return on investment (ROI), reduce total cost of ownership (TCO), and provide the significant business-oriented goals of performance and scale-in, scale-up, and scale-out capacity. Starting with the above essential criteria, it will highlight the key deciding factors in selecting such a solution and then present the key indicator checklist towards a final pick for such a solution implementation. Gartner's Magic Quadrant for Business Intelligence and Analytic Platforms 2014 *positions Oracle as a leader* in the BI and analytic platforms industry (https://www.gartner.com/doc/2668318/magic-quadrant-business-intelligence-analytics). And Oracle Essbase and OBIEE offer a plethora of analytical, tactical, operational, pervasive, and self-service BI capabilities that fit into the usage landscape of customer, business-user, developer, and architect. For a general discussion of Oracle BI, please refer to the website provided in Reference 1.[1] For a BI solution that yields a better business value, please refer to the paper in Reference 2.[2] This can be used as a guideline for the content in Sections 4.2, 4.3, and 4.4.

4.2 Essential Criteria for Requirements Analysis of Oracle Essbase and OBIEE as a Comprehensive BI Solution

The essential criteria categorized in the introduction can be further dissected so as to enable requirements analysis for the design and development of an Oracle Essbase and OBIEE-based BI solution as well as helping to choose the right tools for the right job. Table 4.1 shows an example of how such a list might look.

4.2.1 Business Processes—Discovery and Definition

This primarily involves:

- Determination of the key business rules and processes for the BI solution in the context of both the enterprise and its customers thereof.

Table 4.1 Essential Criteria for an Oracle Essbase and OBIEE-Based Complete BI Solution

Category	Criteria
Business Processes Discovery and Definition	Business process analysis and definition from an analytical and operational standpoint
Information Integration	Data sources involved
	Data integration
Information Dissemination Information Transformation Information Visualization	Type of analysis, reporting, and distribution thereto
Information Visualization User Interaction Information Customization	Information availability and accessibility options
Information in Action User Interaction	Range of analytics: data-centric, customer-centric, cross-process, self-service, and advanced analytics (subjective, prescriptive, and predictive)
Information Customization	Ability to leverage existing infrastructure
Information in Action	Going Beyond BI: Competitive, social, mobile, and cloud intelligence
Information and Big Data	Big Data

- A clear and concise definition of what each process translates to when implemented, taking into consideration the subprocesses, if any, and the primary users of the solution. This enables to prioritize them in order of relevance.
- Understanding existing business processes that pertain to online analytical processing (OLAP) and BI and creating and/or extracting definitive business rules from them.

Doing this eases the procedure of identifying changing business needs and translating them into business processes as well as choose the right BI tools that best-fit into each process, resulting in a solution that is business process driven, value based and yields right-time results.

4.2.2 Information Integration

This involves the need to converge data from multiple sources into a common information platform that can be further leveraged to define unified information architecture (UIA) for BI. Both extract, transform, and load (ETL) and extract, load, and transform (E-LT) processes, complemented by data storage, metadata management, master data management (MDM), some data mining, and data virtualization techniques to seamlessly integrate structured data with unstructured data from external data sources, can be put to the test so as to result in a blueprint for information integration. Also, information integration comprises data quality measures in place that consist of data profiling, assessment and enhancement, and culminates in measuring data quality. Regarding master data management, hierarchical and cross-dimensional, master data across the global enterprise must be taken into consideration during the design phase of UIA.

> *The best-fit way to do this is to identify how data from each data source will be used enterprise-wide as well as by customers and how well the UIA can be integrated with existing enterprise information systems.*

OBIEE enables such an implementation by way of its Common Enterprise Semantic Model, which enables data from any source and in any format to be transparently turned into a logical model. Such a data model can be integrated into the larger UIA, be used as a data source for Oracle Essbase or OBIEE itself, and even be exported to Oracle BI Publisher for operational reporting. Oracle Data Integrator can also be used to extract data from both Oracle and non-Oracle data sources into data formats that are compatible with OBIEE and Oracle Essbase. Both OBIEE and Oracle Essbase can be used as data stores for further analysis and reporting.

4.2.3 Information Dissemination, Transformation, and Visualization

This criteria involves the analysis, reporting, and distribution of collected information thereto and the integration of visualizations based on the same.

Oracle Essbase supports full-service analysis capabilities for OLAP-based business analysis for decision support systems, web-based reporting, and as an OLAP engine for Hyperion EPM. Its MultiDimensional eXpressions (MDX) and XML/A based access methodology, as opposed to being SQL-based, enables cross-dimensional data access. OBIEE supports right-time and near real-time analysis of operational data. Its BI Publisher component enables presentation of information across business marts along with interactive visualizations of the same. The separation of data queries from the reporting layer allows for customized data content to be disseminated to multiple users dynamically.

4.2.4 User Interaction

This criteria involves functionality that enables the creation of ad hoc queries, custom metrics, contextual integration of data at run-time, on-the-fly dynamic visualizations and dashboards, and search capabilities that extend beyond the prebuilt filters.

Oracle BI Answers enables ad hoc querying using data-driven column-level information. Oracle BI Applications allow user interaction by providing users with the flexibility to create self-service business metrics on top of the prepackaged BI solutions. Oracle BI Publisher allows interactive querying of operational data and its seamless integration into OBIEE or export to external formats such as Microsoft Office and PDF files. Oracle Endeca Information Discovery allows self-service information discovery and new search metrics to be defined and integrated as search key performance indicators (KPIs) for the Oracle-based BI solution both at the metadata and analysis levels. Also, OBIEE 11g enables greater dashboard interactivity via drag-and-drop custom data integration and dynamic dashboarding for the end user and improved data visualization.

4.2.5 Information Customization

Regarding the capabilities needed to leverage existing infrastructure, the most significant of them is the ability to reuse existing business processes in place for building new or augmenting existing solutions. The business rules extracted from existing BI processes, as described in the section "Business Process Identification and Definition," can be integrated into the proposed BI solution design to enable a seamless integration with existing IT solutions.

OBIEE enables such an implementation by way of the OBIEE Action Framework, which enables invocation of these business processes from within dashboards and reports. This boils down to turning insight into actions. This ability can be further enhanced to augment information customization and improvisation. Users can then run these reports directly against Oracle BI Server, can use OBIEE as a data source for Essbase, or can export the dashboards in context to Excel for offline use. A data source for the former allows self-service BI by way of a feedback loop into the BI application in context that incorporates the same as BI rules to improvise and auto-generate better decisions using the BI dashboard.

In the implementation stage, this boils down to the customer recognizing the potential of a better business value, not only in terms of TCO/ROI by

> *making use of existing infrastructure, but also in terms of customer lifecycle value (CLV).*

OBIEE also allows personalized BI environments by way of custom views of data based on logical queries built on using any data source, data and format, and dashboards. Such views are database and data-source agnostic and can be r-used across the presentation layer of the BI Solution. Personalized reports based on custom metrics can be built to slice and dice, drill-down, drill-across, and drill-through to a specified grain of data. Additionally, it secures all of this using multiple layers of security.

4.2.6 Information in Action: BI, Advanced Analytics, and Beyond BI (Competitive, Social, and Cloud-Based Intelligence)

This criteria involves processes and corresponding technologies that can be incorporated into the BI solution so as to support insight-driven analysis and analytics. Starting with compare-and-contrast analysis, forecasting, and trend analysis; continuing to prebuilt analytics, advanced analytics comprising new KPIs, dashboards, proactive and predictive analytics; and extending to competitive, social, and cloud-based BI, it is all information in action.

> *Cloud-based BI solution comes with on-demand capacity, elastic capability, extreme performance, mobility, and transparency. A hybrid cloud–based implementation of the same solution provides the additional benefits of security of proprietary data in the private cloud and the elastic benefits of public cloud. It can also enable custom solution for BI-on-the go.*

OBIEE and Oracle Essbase support all of this using Oracle Advanced Analytics, Oracle BI Applications, Oracle Exalytics, and Oracle RightNow Analytics Cloud Service.

4.2.7 Information and Big Data

This involves processes and technologies to best-fit unstructured and semi-structured data into the unified information architecture so as to enable analysis and analytics on the same. Big Data generally includes machine-generated data to identify patterns and correlations, Web-based log data and clickstream data that is huge in volume and generated at high speed. Oracle Exalytics and its inherent Oracle BI Foundation Suite enable processing of Big Data by way of enabling corresponding metadata patterns to be cached in-memory and processed efficiently to achieve high performance. Oracle Exalytics can be run on commodity hardware, easing its integration with the rest of the existing BI environment. Also Oracle Big Data Appliance can be used to analyze and derive insights from Big Data.

4.3 Key and Critical Deciding Factors in Selecting Such a Solution

After studying the essential criteria as presented in section 4.2, the primary factors in deciding an Oracle Essbase– and OBIEE-based BI solution are listed as follows:

- Building a business process view of various business processes, both existing and new, in defining the scope of the BI solution—and involving all concerned business users—from stakeholders to customers.
- Building a business view of data that aligns both business and IT processes from an analysis and BI standpoint, using business terminology in context. This also involves deriving transformations on data that are process-driven.
- Building a logical view of data that encompasses the enterprise landscape. This could include master data and reference data in context, in addition to the transactional and historical data involved. Also, such a view must have the ability to meet the changing data landscape to accommodate multiformat and Big Data requirements. This also involves deriving transformations on data that are data-driven.
- Building a metadata model that allows addition of new data sources on the fly and integration thereof. OBIEE can accommodate multiple heterogeneous data sources in one metadata model.
- Building analytics model tailored towards processing of data factored by *volume, variety, velocity, validity, virtualization,* and *value.* This must have the ability to discover patterns in large-volume and multiformat data and pre-emptive handling of data growth for increased performance.
- Building BI Views that align one-on-one with enterprise lines of business and reporting off each one of them. Ad hoc reports using OBIEE Analysis vis-à-vis subject areas can also be based on these BI Views.
- Building performance management views tailored towards specific business functions comprising of scorecards, performance metrics, event-driven metrics, and performance management dashboards that output

recommendations and can be monitored in right time. The recommendations can then be integrated into the BI solution as business rules, transformations, or analytics to improve information quality and value.

- Building a secure search view of all data in content and context that allows for custom filters and enables on-the-fly search criteria to be specified.

- Building a secure view of the end-to-end solution for information accessibility and availability. This must implement column-level security for user login–based data access to specific columns; row-level security for slicing of data based on appropriate privileges and metrics is based on these slices.

- Building governance, risk, and compliance view of the unified information architecture involved and its use thereof. At the forefront of this is having a robust data quality and master data management methodology. Additionally, this involves proper usage tracking to determine which user is accessing what data, why, and the audit (if the same).

- Building a BI-on-the-go solution and build-your-own-BI (BYOBI) solutions to render the same BI experience on multiple (mobile) devices:
  ○ By leveraging virtualization at the Information Integration, Access, Availability, and BI Presentation layers
  ○ By using BI Solution in the Cloud
  ○ By using Oracle Mobile BI HD

4.4 The Final Pick is a Customer-Centric Solution: Key Indicator Checklist

The Key Indicator Checklist consists of a best practice BI solution design model based on OBIEE and Oracle Essbase that can be used as a reference model. Here's a compilation of the same based on the essential requirements and critical deciding factors in sections 4.2 and 4.3, respectively:

1. Isolation of the data integration (including MDM and metadata management) and data dissemination layers from the business analysis, BI, and business analytics layers, by way of data models that are relational OLAP (ROLAP)– and multidimensional OLAP (MOLAP)–based. ROLAP-based (star schema) and MOLAP-based (MDX cube schema) models can be defined in Oracle Essbase, which in turn can be used as sources for OBIEE, at the same time maintaining the seamless interoperability between the two. Oracle Essbase even allows export of these data models to reuse them at a later time.

2. Design of a data warehouse that has the star schemas and aggregate tables based on it and the MDX cube schemas to leverage multidimensional

data aggregation. OBIEE uses intelligence to select the right aggregates to service the right query and present the information requested to the report/dashboard.

3. Design of the solution based on the UIA, comprising data virtualization, in-memory analytics, adaptive access control, dynamic streaming, and self-service–enabled interactivity and responsiveness. This helps implement a scale-out and scale-up analytical and operational BI solution that aligns with business, IT, and customer demands. Oracle BI Foundation Suite and Oracle BI Solution-in-a-Box allow such a design.

4. Design of a methodology to implement the UIA at each business unit level of the enterprise as well as at the customer-facing application level if required. This must consist of an analysis component that needs to identify the correct data integration strategy based on the actual data itself—across all data touch points.

5. Design of logical queries against the logical view of data using "logical SQL" that can be translated into physical queries. This can also involve applying appropriate data integration techniques, such as ETL, EL-T, data federation, or data virtualization.

6. Design of enhanced functionality for already existing queries by power users to enrich their BI experience.

7. Using the same design and building upon it for adaptability, extensibility, and fine-grained customer visibility, thus taking it beyond intelligence. This is possible by using Oracle Advanced Analytics and self-service–based KPIs as well as dynamic dashboarding—all supported by OBIEE and Oracle Exalytics.

8. Using an "open" design model by being flexible enough to use the same as a reference model that is business-driven and customer-centric, thereby minimizing IT intervention. The ROLAP and MOLAP data models outlined in point 1 can be exported as vendor-neutral design models that can be used as a source for offline and external BI and analysis.

9. Design of a high-performance data visualization platform that leverages the new features of OBIEE 11g and is sourced from a centralized repository of data. Auto-aggregation of multidimensional data and auto-selection from the same for fine-grained BI queries and hierarchical queries.

10. Securing of the end-to-end BI solution using a security and compliance model that adheres GRC principles of business in context. This must allow for prebuilt and custom metrics for identity and access management by way of multifactor authentication and authorization for information availability and accessibility.

11. Managing data as an asset, from data discovery to data as an analytics component encompassing all data from business process view to MDM to BI Views to user-input data. The OBIEE Server, repository, BI catalog, and

Oracle Essbase ensure all BI objects and data are governed and compliant with regulatory standards throughout the lifecycle of the BI solution.

12. Design of an Enterprise Performance Management (EPM) platform that does root cause analysis, which in turn can be used to derive KPIs resulting in performance metrics. Both the root cause and its solution metrics can either be prepackaged as performance analytics or used on a custom basis—and integrated into the complete BI solution.

13. Design of a Mobile BI Solution using Oracle BI Mobile HD, Oracle BI Foundation Suite, or Oracle RightNow Cloud Service.

4.5 Summary

This chapter outlined the essential criteria for requirements analysis of an Oracle Essbase and OBIEE-based complete BI solution, starting from business process analysis to information integration to information transformation and delivery to BI and analytics. It then examined the key critical and deciding factors in selecting such a solution, followed by the final checklist towards a customer-centric solution. The primary focus was on how such a solution can deliver business value and ease decision making in the process. The next chapter will cover Oracle Essbase Data Sources implementation and customization.

4.6 References

1. "Oracle BI: Business Intelligence." Oracle website: http://www.oracle.com/bi.
2. Laura Burkamper, "A Value-Added Approach to Implementing Business Intelligence Solutions." August 2013; http://mcgladrey.com/content/dam/mcgladrey/pdf/wp_value_added_approach_implementing_business_intelligence_solutions.pdf.

Chapter 5

Data Integration, Implementation, and Customization Using Essbase

In This Chapter

5.1 Introduction

As a core component of Oracle's BI technology stack and as a middle-tier online analytical processing (OLAP) server, Oracle Essbase plays a pivotal role for multidimensional analysis across the enterprise spectrum, from data sourcing to data management.

This chapter will examine the data integration component of Oracle Essbase's capabilities, starting from data source definition to consolidation and further customization of the same; semantic integration between Oracle Business Intelligence Enterprise Edition (OBIEE) and Essbase; and extending and customization of Essbase. For a general discussion of Oracle BI, please refer to the websites stated in Reference 1 and 5, and for Essbase, please refer to the website stated in Reference 6.[1,5,6]

5.2 Building an Integrated Approach for Data

Oracle Essbase, as a middle-tier OLAP solution enables data source management using a structured approach for data consolidation. Oracle Essbase Studio is a single tool that can handle heterogeneous data sources from definition to consolidation to administration and customization.

Traditionally, these functions were carried out using Essbase Integration Services and Essbase Administration Services. With the previous tools, the processes involved were quite complex and difficult to handle. Essbase Studio provides a user-friendly toolset for doing all of the data integration needed for Essbase.

> *Using Essbase Studio is the way to go for performing all data integration in Essbase. It is not only easy but also flexible enough to extend Essbase, as will be pointed out in the section "Extending and Customization of Essbase."*

Here's a list highlighting the functionality and tools that enable the same in Oracle Essbase:

- Business rules can be associated with data files while loading. Multiple rules file(s) can be applied to multiple data files identified for loading.
- Any relational database management system (RDBMS) can be used as a data source with its eXtending OLAP (XOLAP) on relational database feature. Using this, the ability to dynamically source from an RDBMS enables data sourcing using a SQL-friendly data retrieval processes.
- Hierarchical data can be sourced using wizards that autocreate the appropriate hierarchies. As an example, using the Time Dimension Wizard enables autocreation of time hierarchies with Essbase Aggregate Storage Option (ASO) databases.
- Data from flat files and Excel spreadsheets can be sourced into Essbase as input to cubes modeling.
- Teradata as a data source can be handled by way of setting the connection properties in the Oracle Essbase server.properties configuration file.

- Oracle OCI connect identifiers and Open Database Connectivity (ODBC) Data Source Names can be used as a data loading interface for handling Oracle and heterogeneous data sources in addition to the default ODBC Essbase connection string dynamically constructed.
- Metadata objects such as dimensions, data sources, and lists (including text lists) can be reused using the common metadata repository via the Essbase Studio catalog and at the lowest detail of granularity. This catalog can be exported or imported into an XML file for offline usage. Furthermore, data source analysis can be done in an "online" fashion without locking the catalog.
- Mini-schemas can be defined paired directly with data source connections.
- Data Source connections to Oracle Real Application Cluster (RAC) sources can be defined and customized. The Connection Wizard allows for specification of multiple Oracle RAC sever nodes per connection based on an Oracle Service Name.
- Essbase Server Clusters can be used as a data source, with Essbase Studio allowing definition of the same.
- Essbase data source connections can be kept in "live" sync with the underlying physical connections by way of deletion or refresh operations on the physical data source changes or schema alterations. This can be done Delete and Refresh table commands in the Data Sources tab of the Source Navigator in Essbase Studio.

Figure 5.1 shows a high-level view of Oracle Essbase Data Source Implementation along with End User Interface.

5.2.1 Recommendations

To get a holistic view of using Oracle Essbase in the enterprise, the authors suggest the following as best-fit scenarios for its implementation:

1. Use Essbase standalone, as a source for analytical BI. This is shown in Figure 5.1 as a directive from "Heterogeneous Data Sources" to "Oracle Essbase." Analytical BI goes beyond traditional reporting to support forward-looking analytics, "what-if" analysis and scenario modeling. The special Oracle Hyperion Smart View for Office integration allows this to be done at the enterprise level and in a scalable and intuitive way.

   Based on the data sources, dimensions, facts, measures, and the like can be configured in Essbase.

Business Intelligence and Analytics

- Reporting
- Dashboards
- Delivery/Scheduling

- Cube Developer
- Querying Tool
- Analytics

Cubes

Relational Databases

DW

ODS

Data Integration

Common Enterprise Information Model

Misc. Sources (e.g. files, spreadsheets)

Misc. Databases

Operational Data

Data Sources

Figure 5.1 High-Level View of Oracle Essbase Data Cubes Implementation. (Reproduced with permission from BIS3 LLC © 2015.)

2. Use Essbase against a data warehouse/star schema that forms a common enterprise information model. This introduces a data repository in the Essbase catalog structured as a star schema that inherently populates it in a definitive manner used for querying performance. This repository serves as a single version of the truth—an advantage of a common model thereto. This is indicated by the lines from "Heterogeneous Data Sources" to "Oracle DB/DW" to "Oracle Essbase" in Figure 5.1.

3. Use Essbase as an in-memory accelerator for Oracle Exalytics that leverages the next-generation data architecture of in-memory computing. This functionality is available as of 2014 and optimizes cube-based analyses in-memory. (For further information the reader is advised to refer to the Oracle White Paper: "Oracle Exalytics In-Memory Machine: A Brief Introduction."[4])

5.3 Implementation Specifics of Data, from Data Source to Data Analytics

Oracle Essbase implementation follows certain specifics in order to source data from multiple sources and output data as intelligence and analytics with value added to what was raw data. The following is a brief list of the same:

- Data source connections
- Metadata source connections
- Mini-schemas
- Metadata elements like dimensions, attribute-based members, etc.
- Hierarchies
- Cube schemas
- Cubes and Essbase models (that include Essbase Server connections)

The following paragraph describes in a nutshell how to implement these specifics in Essbase. For detailed information on how to go about creating and maintaining the same, the reader is recommended to check Oracle's online documentation *Oracle Essbase 11.1.2—Oracle by Example*[2] and *Oracle Essbase Studio 11.1.2 Product Overview*.[3]

The technology platform underlying an Oracle Essbase solution encompasses in-memory data store, in-database processing, mobile, and cloud (build your own data source). Oracle Essbase separates OLAP from OLTP, thereby ensuring faster analytical queries on large datasets while maintaining optional OLTP subsecond response time. The Oracle Essbase platform enables compression that's configurable based on *data store (aka data source)* and *workload*.

A quick implementation overview using Essbase Studio is as follows:

1. Establish connections to the data sources using the Connection Wizard. The Connection Wizard is intelligent enough to identify the data source type and display the appropriate specifications input fields for each such type.
2. Using multiple data sources and metadata sources:
   a. Build metadata elements such as dimensions, date elements, derived text measures, and alias tables using either the Create metadata elements tab in the Connection Wizard or the Metadata Navigator.
   b. Build hierarchies—standard, measure, parent-child, shared member or alternate roll-up, and calendar hierarchy types. Specialized hierarchies such as those with added attribute dimensions and varying attributes based can also be created. The Hierarchy Editor can be used for this step. A folder must first be created or selected in the Metadata Navigator.
   c. Build (cube) schemas using Cube Schema Wizard, specifying dimensions, measures, and hierarchies for the same. Mini-schemas can be defined too, based on enhanced functionality of data source connections. Mini-schemas can be defined in the Connection Wizard. Data load mappings can be specified in this step.
3. Build Essbase models from cube schemas. Set appropriate properties for the model, including dimension and other member properties such as data load bindings. Essbase Models can be created from Cube Schema Wizard.
4. Consolidate the above built Essbase data structures by storing them in the Essbase catalog. These can be reused to generate Essbase cubes just-in-time or at a later point in time.
5. Set Essbase configuration and server properties using the essbase.cfg and server.properties files. A wide range of settings can be configured to improve and optimize the data source definition, consolidation, and data load processes. Properties can also be set for cubes deployment.
6. Generate Essbase outlines using the above settings and initiate the dimension and data load processes.
7. Deploy Essbase Cubes using Cube Deployment Wizard.

5.4 Semantic Integration between OBIEE and Essbase, Using OBIEE as a Data Source for Oracle Essbase

OBIEE can be used as a data provider for Essbase in two ways:

1. Use the OBIEE presentation layer
2. Use the OBIEE Business Model layer

Additionally, the tight integration of Oracle BI Foundation Suite with Oracle Essbase provides write-back capability to the Essbase cubes from OBIEE and Essbase as Aggregate Persistence target. This feature is unique in that Essbase allows this not only to Essbase cubes but also to an application's data repository and enabling the users to do this while maintaining security via application roles and policies. The aggregations done in OBIEE can be stored in Essbase ASO cubes that can be queried using SQL and/or MDX functions that are mapped to equivalent Essbase MDX functions.

Additionally, Essbase Model and cube schema creation can be done during the data source connection definition process using Essbase Studio. The Essbase Model can be based on the OBIEE Business Model in context. Oracle Essbase Studio allows connections to OBIEE, directly thereby facilitating cube creation using OBIEE as a data source. On another note, OBIEE dimensions can be created from Essbase Studio.

> *Use OBIEE as a data source for Oracle Essbase when there is a need to tie MDX analytical capabilities to operational BI and thereby obtain an alignment of operational business processes with reporting and analytical BI. This also allows for scalability across a broader range of data sources and user base.*

5.4.1 Recommendations

To get a holistic view of using OBIEE as a data source for Essbase, the authors suggest the following as best-fit scenarios for its implementation:

1. To leverage existing relational BI functionality within the enterprise and use it for Essbase-based OLAP, use the OBIEE Semantic Model to load data from it into Essbase cubes via data access using federated queries in OBIEE. The full integration of OBIEE and Oracle Essbase enables this.
2. To improve the performance of analytical BI and hybrid OLAP (HOLAP), in terms of speed and multidimensional analysis, use OBIEE's *write-back capability to Essbase Cubes*. This functionality allows *cube spin-off* based on retrieval of subsets of data (e.g., by subject area in OBIEE) extracted from the BI dashboard or RPD; one can spin it off as an Essbase ASO or Block Storage Option (BSO) cube and perform auto-analysis

against it. This also creates an Essbase analysis target. OBIEE's logical SQL "CREATE CUBE" declarative command is generated; it is completely based on OBIEE presentation layer objects. Per Oracle,[5] once the CREATE CUBE command is executed within OBIEE, the cube can be edited within Essbase and resolved to aggregate across chosen or all levels of its dimensions. The cube also allows duplicate member names for its dimensions and levels. The Essbase analysis created can be mapped into the RPD physical layer and also can act as Business Model logical table source for the OBIEE logical data model.

3. To optimize OBIEE Business Model performance in terms of query response time and answers, source data from the Business Model in OBIEE and load it into Essbase, improvise the corresponding cube to fit in relational OLAP (ROLAP), multidimensional OLAP (MOLAP), and HOLAP, and remap the OBIEE Business Model to use the Essbase cube as the data source instead of the existing relational sources.

The above three options are diagrammatically represented in Figure 5.2.

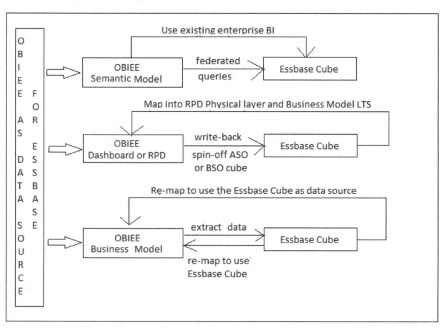

Figure 5.2   Options for Using OBIEE as Oracle Essbase Data Source

5.4.2 Implementation Specifics

The implementation specifics for the above options involve using Essbase Studio, and Essbase Administration Services and OBIEE.

For option (1) from the recommendations above, the steps involved using Essbase Studio are as follows:

1. Define a new data source connection and reference it in OBIEE. The data source type in the Connection Wizard in Essbase Studio must be specified as OBIEE.
2. If the appropriate relational data model is not inherited from OBIEE, this needs to be defined in Essbase Studio, using a Schema in the Metadata Navigator.
3. Define the necessary hierarchies for dimensions and measures along with the appropriate source elements, if any (as defined in OBIEE), in the Metadata Navigator. This can include ragged as well as value-based hierarchies.
4. Create a new Cube Schema based on the dimensions (regular hierarchies) and facts (measure hierarchies) in the Metadata Navigator and Cube Schema Wizard. Here you can also specify transformations for dimension member names, aliases, and aggregation rules. It may be necessary to specify the Cube Type as ASO. This enables auto-aggregation of data on demand.
5. Create a new Essbase Model based on the Cube Schema.
6. Validate the Essbase Cube Model and deploy it to create the cube, build the outline, and load the cube, using the Cube Deployment Wizard from the Metadata Navigator. The outline is visible from within Essbase and can be previewed to validate its data for aggregation.

For option (2) in this list, the implementation specifics have been described in the same.

For option (3) in this list, the Essbase cube built from the OBIEE Semantic Model can be reverse-engineered into OBIEE to serve as a MDX data source in the OBIEE logical model. It can either add to the OBIEE relational structures or replace an already existing traditional data source in OBIEE. It can also be customized to add aliases and dimension member names to map to the descriptions in the logical model. Also, further analysis can be done based on this cube (across all levels and aggregations defined in the cube), using MDX for ASO cubes and Essbase code script for BSO cubes.

5.4.3 Using OBIEE 12c for Essbase 12c

Throughout this book, the authors have stressed using a logical (dimensional) model to define the dimensions and facts needed to build Essbase Cubes as well as using ROLAP/MOLAP schemas to extend Essbase for custom analytics and analytical BI.

Oracle recently released OBIEE 12c and with it, included Essbase 12c as an inherent component. There are three major components, as follows:

BI Enterprise Edition—the main BI product
BI Publisher—for pixel-perfect professional formatted reports
Essbase—via the Essbase BI Accelerator Wizard for user-driven reporting

The Essbase12c option is a new component of OBIEE 12c and can be accessed via the new "Essbase Business Intelligence Acceleration Wizard." This can be used to build Essbase cubes based on facts and dimensions directly from the RPD. It enables interactive querying of the RPD and determination of dimension hierarchies and data sources. Essbase ASO can be built from it, and the dimensions and data can be loaded and the RPD configured to use all of these.

The Essbase 12c option has a Java agent and an Essbase Server integrated into OBIEE 12c.

According to Oracle, "The Essbase RBDMS schema is the Oracle relational database that stores the Essbase application and database metadata (when Essbase is deployed on a WebLogic Server Cluster)." In addition, "The Essbase agent connects to Essbase RDBMS schema using Eclipse Link, an open source mapping and persistence framework. The Essbase server connects to the Essbase RDBMS schema using ODBC DataDirect drivers."[7]

The Essbase Admin Console and Essbase Studio are no longer available in Essbase 12c. Custom cubes can be built from a standalone installation of Essbase and Essbase Studio and can be imported into OBIEE 12c, as is the case in OBIEE 11g, but this involves a completely separate installation and configuration.

This new architecture of OBIEE 12c along with Essbase 12c is along similar lines as the logical (dimensional) model in Essbase Studio (described throughout this book), and it can be utilized to use OBIEE as a source for Essbase. For further reading, the authors recommend the following websites: https://docs.oracle.com/cd/E66975_01/doc.1221/essbase_db.pdf, http://www.redstk.com/installing-obiee-12c-part-4-configuring-starting-obiee/, and http://john-goodwin.blogspot.com/2015/11/essbase-12c-for-bi-glimpse-into-future.html?m=1.

5.5 Extending and Customizing Essbase

The Oracle BI Suite, consisting of BI Publisher, OBIEE, and Essbase, constitutes a toolset for holistic BI and analytics. This boils down to using BI Publisher for operational reporting, OBIEE for operational BI, and Essbase for multidimensional analysis and analytical BI.

Initially, Siebel was missing MOLAP analysis, which is why Oracle bought Hyperion for MOLAP. The seamless integration between Essbase and OBIEE enables transparent integration between the two, thus enabling extension of Essbase cubes to be flexible, efficient, and scalable. This section will cover extension and customization of Essbase from the following two perspectives:

- Extension of Essbase cubes
- Analytics that can be applied to custom implementations

5.5.1 Extending Essbase Cubes

Extending Essbase cubes is useful in implementations that already use Essbase for analysis/analytics (and OBIEE in certain cases). This can be done by using a data mart in the cube itself or using a ROLAP data warehouse star schema in an RDBMS *that feeds the cube.*

> *We stress that the ROLAP star schema in the RDBMS is equivalent to the dimensional model in Essbase.*

As mentioned above, extending Essbase cubes can be done using either of the following ways:

1. Using a data mart included in the cube itself (as a dimensional model specifying dimensions and their measures).
2. Using a ROLAP star schema in an RDBMS, more specifically sourced from an enterprise data warehouse (EDW), thus conforming to the single version of truth. The EDW itself is a star.

> *In either case, we need to go through the process of putting a dimensional model that mirrors business requirements (at least on paper). This must involve business users and IT to sit across the board and chalk out specific business requirements that get mapped to equivalent technical steps for the dimensional model. This is needed for the translation of the star one-on-one with the mapped end user requirements..*

5.5.1.1 When To Use What

First we state the preferred way to a holistic approach for extending Essbase and BI.

> *The preferred way to a holistic solution is to design an EDW based on OLTP requirements and have Essbase source data directly from the EDW via XOLAP or using ROLAP star. This allows for performing operational reporting/publishing, analytical BI and operational BI.*

Option 1 in the previous section can be used if there is a unique need to cater to a department that needs to perform MOLAP/analytics and not just flat reporting. XOLAP can be used as the technology to directly and transparently source the data from OLTP/RDBMS and feed the cube via the dimensional model in Essbase Studio.

Option 2 can be used if there is a need for reporting as opposed to analytics. In this case, the ROLAP star can be used to feed the cube via the logical dimensional model in Essbase studio.

Note that in either case the logical dimensional model does not necessarily mean a logical data model. This may mean that a data mart might not physically reside in the cube but exists as an equivalent MOLAP cube.

The steps involving in building a cube in Essbase Studio based on a ROLAP star are as follows:

1. Design a ROLAP model (star schema)
2. Design a data connection based on this ROLAP model
3. Design an Essbase cube based on the ROLAP star created in step 1. This way, the ROLAP feeds the data to the cube.
4. Repeat step 3 for any similar cubes that need to be designed based on members of the Essbase outline or any additional dimensions/measures from the ROLAP model
5. Design an Essbase model based on this cube
6. Deploy the cube

> *Recommendation: Use these two options explained in the prior section to extend the existing cubes, build additional cubes that can be built, and perform analytics. This is very flexible.*

Figure 5.3 depicts how Essbase can be extended and analytics can be applied to custom implementations.

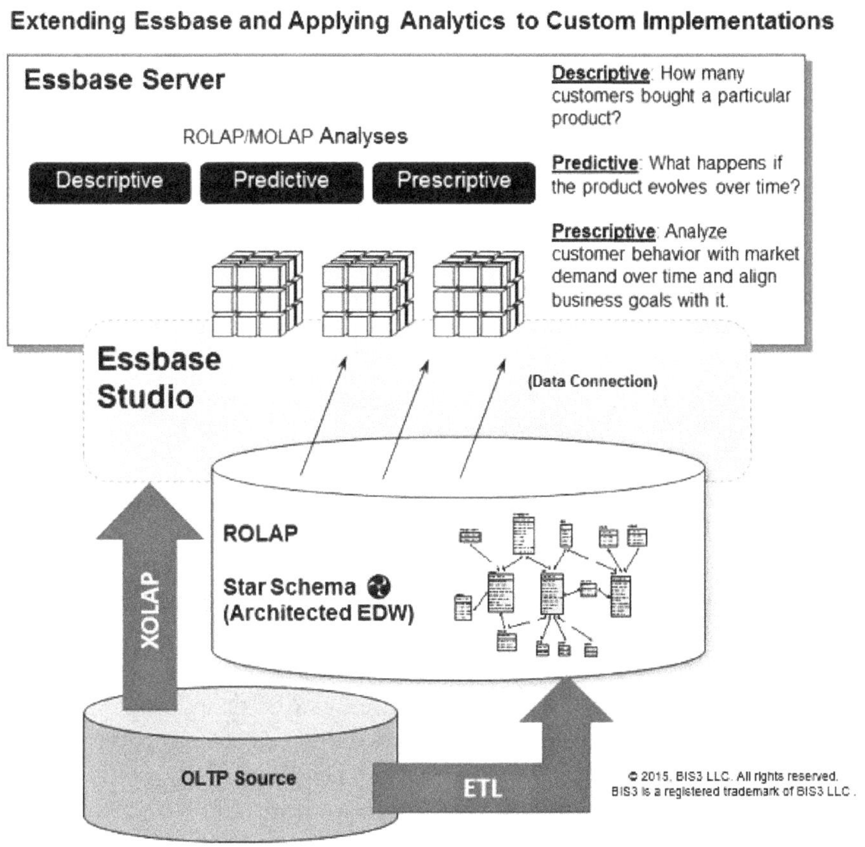

Figure 5.3 Extending Essbase and Applying Analytics to Custom Implementations. (Reproduced with permission from BIS3 LLC © 2015.)

5.5.2 Analytics That Can Be Applied to Custom Implementations

Extending Essbase cubes using a ROLAP dimensional model as outlined in the prior subsection provides the way to go for determining what kind of analytics that can be done to apply to custom implementations. A choice of techniques as described in subsection 5.5.1.1 can also be used to perform analytics as applicable.

5.5.2.1 Recommendations

The authors recommend the following process for applying analytics to custom Essbase implementations:

1. *Perform hybrid online transaction processing (OLTP)/OLAP analytics*: Start with a ROLAP dimensional model to represent particular business processes that need the final analytics as actionable insights. This leads to an integrated approach, by which we have analyzed what is ad hoc reporting (BI Publisher) and operational BI (OBIEE) using ROLAP through star schema, and multidimensional analysis (in Essbase) for MOLAP/ analytical BI. This is the right foundation that gives a holistic solution.

> Do the dimensional logical ROLAP model outside of Essbase Studio. This is a better way. As a first exercise, this can be done as a prototype in Essbase Studio and then formally industrialized outside of Essbase Studio. This is a fantastic process that enables direct connectection to transactional OLTP systems and also uses analytical data to do hybrid analytics.

2. *Perform descriptive, predictive, and prescriptive analytics*: As an extension of step 1, customization of Essbase via ROLAP models and integration into Essbase enables us to perform BI and Advanced Analytics at the same time. This means doing *descriptive analytics on data from transactional (OLTP) systems and predictive analytics (what's now, and what if)* from both OLTP and OLAP systems with subsecond response times. The latter can be done using Essbase BSO cubes. The former can be done using ASO cubes, which are efficient and scalable across thousands of concurrent users. The outcomes from predictive analytics can be enhanced to derive *prescriptive analytics (what's next)* that provide recommendations for actionable decision making. Predictive analytics can be done in the following manner:

    a. Define dimension hierarchies corresponding to business structures such as business dimensions. This can be standardized as "scenario" dimensions.

    b. Based on what's current (e.g., trending and similar occurrences), derive what-if rules that can be ranked based on likelihood and closeness to the business process involved.

    c. Create data that models the what-if scenarios and outcomes that align with what's next.

    d. Try and incorporate the predictive model as a standard business process using multi-user read/write capabilities and the write-back feature of Essbase.

5.5.3 Best Practices and Additional Customization Scenarios

This section outlines some best practices and additional customization scenarios of using Essbase in the enterprise.

- Leverage Essbase Studio's functionality to implement data integration that facilitates change. Essbase Studio supports sourcing from a data warehouse (in ROLAP form) and populating the Essbase cube. Alternately, a part of the data warehouse can be used as data mart to source the Essbase cube. This takes care of manageability, scalability, flexibility, and extensibility in regard to sourcing data and stuffing the Essbase cube because of the relational structure of the data warehouse. The warehouse also enables to have change data capture and incremental data loads.

> *Do not use Essbase for ETL or E-LT type processes—for targeted output that requires minimal re-engineering and changes or provides the flexibility to accommodate current data as well future data. Facts and dimensions required can be modeled in the data warehouse for data aggregations, and any other analyses can be defined and redefined based on current and future requirements, thus making the data integration process change-proof and part of the holistic Essbase and OBIEE solution.*

- The primary input for Oracle Essbase is data, and all data needs to be validated at the time of sourcing from the data veracity, integrity, and quality points of view. The following list comprises tasks recommended to be done at the data warehouse layer. There are three aspects in which data can be used for best results:
  ○ Use load first, and then check and transform.
  ○ Use data validation as part of the workflow in the data warehouse, not only to ensure data is fully validated during sourcing data, but also to enable a consistent set of pertinent data for the cause of which it is used. This enables the filtration of data that won't be loaded. Automating this process removes the complexities involved in the process.
  ○ Eliminate bad data by checking that:
    ▪ The data source and data process are consistent
    ▪ Exceptions have been taken care of
    ▪ Data is completed and validated to its source
    ▪ Data is completed and validated for dimensions and facts
    ▪ The automated workflow is functioning without any errors or data spills that are outliers
- Use Essbase custom-defined functions for calculations to extend Essbase's calculation functions.
- Use Essbase to leverage a single analytic platform that integrates disparate information for yielding better business decisions. Essbase Studio can be used to do this at the data source level, and Essbase cubes can be built on the same via a MOLAP data model to push analytics needed. This can be

used to produce real-time (in fact right-time) reports either using Essbase standalone or by integrating it with Oracle BI.

- Use XOLAP cubes in Oracle Essbase Studio, starting with the 11.1.2.4 release, to convert Essbase BSO cubes to Hybrid, and use them in Hyperion applications for Hybrid and Advanced Relational Access. In a way, this optimizes Essbase for Hybrid Analyses. Also, BSO's Hybrid ASO-like aggregation can be used. For example, the Hybrid Engine can be used for cross-dimensional hybrid formulas and Hyperion Planning Applications for gathering real-time insight from data.
- Use SQL as part of the Essbase integration to source data from any data source and integrate data and metadata into Essbase more easily and efficiently. Use SQL queries to load data into Essbase outlines. This process can be automated in Essbase Studio.
- Use BSO and ASO cubes based on data, query and calculation requirements:
  - Use BSO cubes as opposed to ASO cubes for optimized calculations (e.g., to overcome the challenges in stored vs. dynamic hierarchies and dynamic time series–based calculations). Applications using ASO cubes converted to BSO result in better performance when integrated with financial modules for reporting purposes.
  - Use ASO cubes for high-speed data loading, (real-time) aggregations, and faster query response time when the underlying data doesn't involve complex hierarchies and temporal analysis. Also, use ASO cubes in applications that need to scale far beyond the limits of what BSO can offer.
- Use Oracle Data Relationship Governance (DRG) within Data Relationship Management (DRM) to facilitate creation and maintenance of master data. Workflow models, requests, governance work lists, alerts and notifications, and paths can be configured right out of the box within DRM. Using runtime substitution variables calculations for allocations across BSO and ASO cubes can be done so as to make them work together. The corresponding metadata can be synchronized using DRM. Using DRG in a way extends Essbase beyond its normal functionality for governance workflow and approval process by allowing copying of workflow models and tasks, automatic updates for request items, governance of Web Service API, database integration, EPM integration, and external workflow.
- Use Essbase in the Cloud for creating ad hoc grids for enterprise financial users to save them as reports. The same can be done on-premise too.

5.6 Summary

This chapter outlined the data integration, implementation, and customization methodologies in Oracle Essbase. It touched upon defining data sources, dimensions, metadata elements, hierarchies, mini-schemas, cubes and cube schemas, and Essbase models in such an implementation. Next, it described implementing specifics from data sources to data analytics process. The subsequent section outlined using OBIEE as a data source for Essbase. The final section touched upon extending and customization of Essbase cubes. The next chapter will highlight the use of Essbase for analytical BI.

5.7 References

1. "Oracle BI: Business Intelligence." Oracle website: http://www.oracle.com/bi
2. "Oracle Essbase 11.1.2—Oracle by Example" (tutorials). Oracle website: http://www.oracle.com/technetwork/middleware/essbase/tutorials/ess1112-396125.html
3. "Essbase Studio 11.1.2 Product Overview." Oracle website: http://www.oracle.com/webfolder/technetwork/tutorials/tutorial/hyp/EssbaseStudio_11.1.2_Overview/LessonIndex.htm
4. "Oracle Exalytics In-Memory Machine: A Brief Introduction." January 2014. Oracle white paper: http://www.oracle.com/us/solutions/ent-performance-bi/business-intelligence/exalytics-bi-machine/overview/exalytics-introduction-1372418.pdf
5. "Oracle Business Intelligence Enterprise Edition Samples." Oracle website: http://www.oracle.com/technetwork/middleware/bi-foundation/obiee-samples-167534.html
6. "Oracle Essbase." Oracle website: http://www.oracle.com/technetwork/middleware/essbase/overview/index.html
7. "Oracle Essbase Database Administrator's Guide for Release 12.2.1." Oracle website: https://docs.oracle.com/cd/E66975_01/doc.1221/essbase_db.pdf (Chapter 63, pages 927 and 930)

Chapter 6

Using Essbase for Analytical BI

In This Chapter

6.1 Introduction

This chapter will examine the role of Essbase in Analytical BI as a specific component of a comprehensive BI and analytics solution. It begins by identifying what kind of analytical measures are good for Essbase Cubes and continues by highlighting the implementation specifics of analytical BI using Essbase. As part of using Essbase for analytical BI, in additional to analytical reporting, Essbase fills the gap of cube predictive analytics and, when combined with Oracle Business Intelligence Enterprise Edition (OBIEE), provides a holistic solution of a combined OBIEE and Essbase–based implementation.

It is beyond the scope of this book to fully describe and discuss data mining, predictive analytics, and artificial intelligence beyond what are currently used in today's business intelligence (BI) and analytics landscape. BI is setting up the next steps for what we imagine in the future. But in keeping with the theme of this book, we try to establish and define the best practices of BI that will create the foundation of what is to come.

Our book briefly covers the high-level and general principles that we want to adhere to and utilizes Essbase for Analytical BI. For detailed instructions and training, please refer to our instructional website at www.esssbasestudio. com. For a general discussion of Oracle BI, please refer to the website provided in References 1 and 5; for Essbase, please refer to the website provided in References 2, 3, and 6.[1–3, 5, 6]

6.2 What Kind of Analytics Are Good for Essbase Cubes?

Oracle Essbase comes with the ability to handle descriptive analytics that can handle repeatable and expandable data and is scalable across implementations involving hundreds of concurrent users. But some measures enable it to be extended to make it usable for predictive and prescriptive analytics, as shown in Figure 6.1. This figure depicts how Essbase can be extended and analytics can be applied to custom implementations to a certain possible extent.

Here's a bird's eye view of certain practical analytics and queries that make up the before-mentioned categories:

- Descriptive analytics:
  o What were the daily sales of a particular product?
  o How were the sales for the previous day compared to those for the day before?
  o What were the reasons for any discrepancies?
  o What is the sales activity in the last quarter?
  o If the sales were low, what factors led to the low sales activity?
- Predictive analytics:
  o What happens if the product evolves over time?
  o How will the sales trend be in such a situation and why?
- Prescriptive analytics:
  o What measures can be taken to improve poor sales?
  o How can we introduce these measures into existing business processes?

Analytics involving MDX queries, X by X, and online analytical processing (OLAP)-aware queries, planning and forecasting, and financial management can be best handled by Essbase when extended using a DW-based holistic solution that leverages quality data constructs and architecture.

Figure 6.1 shows the realm of Analysis, BI, and Analytics.

The Realm of Reporting and BI for Analysis and Analytics

Cubes

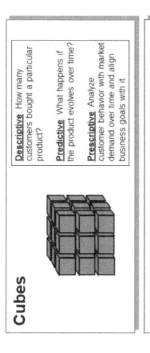

Descriptive: How many customers bought a particular product?

Predictive: What happens if the product evolves over time?

Prescriptive: Analyze customer behavior with market demand over time and align business goals with it.

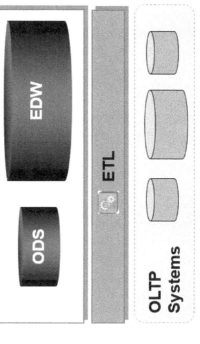

EDW

ODS

ETL

OLTP Systems

Analytical BI

Latency of being nightly

Operational BI

Combination of both nightly and immediate latency.

For near real-time/intraday, report off of ODS

Operational Reporting

Latency of being immediate

Figure 6.1 Realm of Analysis, BI, and Analytics. (Reproduced with permission from BIS3 LLC © 2015.)

6.2.1 Recommendations

To get a holistic view of using Oracle Essbase for analytics, the authors suggest the following:

1. Because the gap of OBIEE renders it unable to fully address predictive analytics, the authors suggest using the analytical power of cubes and multidimensional structures for cube predictive analytics and the functionality of predictive and prescriptive analytics—a holistic solution consisting of OBIEE and Essbase. This helps in accelerating decisions involving what if and what's next, as well as enhancing business performance.

2. Data from multiple sources can be fed into Essbase directly or via a relational OLAP (ROLAP) data warehouse and processed inside the cubes. Different kinds of analytic measures can be derived from them and used for reporting directly or sent to an OBIEE business analytics dashboard for self-service analytics. The key here is how Essbase, as a multidimensional engine, can process data from a variety of sources and turn it into measures that can be built into the solution as analytics for interday reporting. As an example, customer marketing data can be used to derive specific advertising channels' information and analytics can be built upon that data to improvise on market segmentation for descriptive and prescriptive analytics. New data sets can also be created for predictive analytics. The Oracle Exalytics machine for BI can incorporate Essbase as an in-memory accelerator for performing MDX analysis. For further discussion, please refer to the White Paper, "Oracle Exalytics In-Memory Machine: A Brief Introduction."[4]

6.3 Implementation Specifics of Using Analytical BI Using Essbase

Oracle Essbase supports multiple types of implementation methods for Analytical BI. Essbase allows the creation of facts, dimensions, measures, and joins at the time of sourcing data and feeding these into a ROLAP star schema without losing the dimensional granularity and hierarchy levels, so fact-level measures functionality adheres to the dimensional model (e.g., the business model or part thereof). The star schema can then be used as a data source for Essbase.

The following outline some of the recommended methods for the same:

1. Use logical cubes in addition to physical cubes and Cube Materialized Views for analysis. This approach works well when the number of

dimensions is not very high in number; additionally, it does not restrict dimensional access to the data. The underlying implementation technology can be a ROLAP schema architected as a data warehouse or data mart. The combination of ROLAP and in-memory cubes enables subsecond analysis and analytic measures for OLAP-based analysis. Use of aggregations, custom expressions, slicing and dicing, and filtering of data based on dimensions, levels, and measures can be incorporated to derive multidimensional metrics, aggregations and custom calculations that can be applied to data directly in the data warehouse or cube without having to move the data out.

2. Factor in predictive analytics, and the role of Essbase for analytical BI is enhanced with the ability to model complex data sets dynamically using analytical measures for predicting behavior and prescriptive decision support.

Essbase Studio can be used to construct the cubes and design the analytics for Essbase applications for Analytical BI and reporting involving drill-through and drill across.

In a typical Oracle Essbase implementation there might be hundreds of cubes to be managed. As pointed out in Chapter 5, Sections 5.4 and 5.5, we suggested a data warehousing solution that is established for OBIEE: utilize the metadata of OBIEE from the RPD that gives an extra advantage of using enterprise metadata. This data warehouse should be the source for Essbase—the very best tool for Analytical BI that can host data that is expandable and repeatable.

The data warehouse solution eliminates a lot of cubes—it does data cleansing and data quality that a cube cannot do. This way, we can let the data fuel the choice of implementation and not choose the tool merely for the sake of having a tool, based on an unwarranted perceived notion or biased preferences.

6.3.1 Using Essbase for Analytical BI

Oracle Essbase supports analytics in multiple domains by way of reuse of existing cubes. For example, sales analytics using numeric measures can be derived that can provide real-world business solutions. Essbase allows this by sharing existing metadata between cubes, such as dimensions and attributes. Time hierarchy and product hierarchy are two examples that can be reused across domains such as sales and marketing and spending. The existing cube structure can be leveraged to create new analytics for the target domain. Given below is a design strategy of how this can be achieved. All of the below steps can be performed in Essbase Studio. Additionally, the newly created dimensions and measures can be added as extensions to the already existing logical dimensional model.

1. Take into account the existing Time dimensions available, such as Year, Quarter, Month, Week, and Day.
2. Take into account the existing Product dimension.
3. Consider the measures that can be reused, such as Profit pertaining to the product.
4. Take into account the Scenario dimension.
5. Note that all of these already exist in the precreated Essbase outline.
6. Create a new Sales and Marketing cube based on the relevant existing cube. Add child dimensions from the Time hierarchy. For example, Week and Day can be added if they are missing in the existing hierarchy, along with member values. Also add new dimensions to the cube along with corresponding member values.

Ensure that new member names are represented using aliases and reflect business terminology and are unique across the existing and new cubes in the Essbase outline. However, the shared dimensions themselves, such as Product and Time, can have the same name and member values.

---

7. Repeat step 6 for the measures as desired.
8. Prepare the data to be loaded so that it is cleansed and has the correct dimension, attribute, and member names and values. Once this is done, load the data into the cube.
9. Create new analytics based on this new cube that pertain to real-world business analysis. This can be done by utilizing Essbase's ability to filter on existing data based on member selection. And all of this can be done in real time or on-demand. Such analytics can include:
   a. Sales figures by product for current and last month
   b. Profit generated in the current month versus last month by product. This helps in determining the top n products sold by month and in projecting future sales by product
   c. Spend analysis by month by product by marketing campaign to determine how well a product is faring across each month for the marketing campaign used. This can also be used to project future spending for maximum sales as well as up-sell needs.

6.3.2 Using BSO Cubes for Analytical BI

Block Storage Option (BSO) cubes can be used for Analytical BI in the following ways:

1. Adding new data sources by defining connections and adding tables.
2. Modeling text files. (In addition, SmartView for Office allows Essbase to directly interact with Excel for data retrieval and cube navigation purposes.)
3. Modeling data sources by creating mini-schemas. Mini-schemas are first-class objects used to create logical groupings of tables in order to construct a subject area to work with. This is a preliminary step in data modeling using Essbase Studio to create analytic applications. This step is followed by associating tables with the mini-schema. To create the missing joins in the mini-schema panel, a ROLAP star can be a source for the mini-schema, and by specifying/utilizing this, we can have Essbase set up for Analytical BI and reporting.

> *This drill-through capability into a relational data warehouse is a vital feature and functionality of analytics and Analytical BI. Multiple fact tables can be used in the mini-schema and both fact tables and the mini-schema can provide data to the analytic model. In fact, the mini-schema can be modified later to add tables to bring in the data model that may have been modified after creation of mini-schema.*

4. Extending Essbase by creating metadata elements in Essbase Studio. Existing relational columns from data warehousing or custom(er)-created ones, dimensions, fields from a text file, hierarchies, canned drill-through reports or cube schemas, or any other element that can be used in architecting an analytical model can be used to generate new elements or reorganized into hierarchies as well as cross-data sources and data source types. Hierarchies can be created from metadata elements. Dimension elements can be used to form levels within hierarchies or as distinct members. Dimension elements can be organized as families with ascending or descending sort order. Even families can be made part of hierarchies. Custom elements can be created as dimensions by either deriving them from existing elements or by building them using functions such as Time dimension. Essbase cubes can be associated with these custom dimensions while creating analytics or for analytical reporting. Measures and scenarios can also be created as hierarchies. These help in the building process of creating MDX metrics.

5. Using cube schemas. Cube schemas are a set of hierarchies that define the dimensions of a cube. Hierarchies are associated with cube schemas during the cube schema creation process. The steps involved data modeling in Essbase Studio involve the following:

   a. Define the properties in Essbase for dimension, dimension level, or specific member (in case of measures). Aliases can be assigned to hierarchies by creating alias tables and assigning them to the Essbase data/analytic model. Examples include formulae, data consolidation operators, and the like.

   b. Validate the model prior to deployment.

   c. Set deployment options such as Aggregate Storage Option (ASO), BSO, or eXtending OLAP (XOLAP) model. Also, specify the option to include metadata only, data only, or both.

   d. Execute the deployment in the specific Essbase server associated during the data source creation process.

6. Using Essbase for drill-through and drill-back reporting.

7. Using a ROLAP star schema as a data warehouse to feed the Essbase cube. Though Essbase Studio can connect any data source as stated earlier, our approach here pertains to the recommendation of using a ROLAP star schema as a data warehouse to feed the Essbase cube and we point out here the functionality involved for analytical reporting, AKA Analytical BI, based on the ROLAP star as the primary data source. Report content can be defined dynamically from new metrics based on calculations or otherwise from added dimensions and measures. There is no need to refresh drill-through data upon modification of report structure or data source. Dynamic association of reports to Essbase models enables autosynchronization across all appropriate models. Therefore, if the data in the data warehouse changes, or additional dimensions are added to ROLAP schema, these can be carried to the Essbase report, and the data associated with it as well as the modified report structure are available in the corresponding analytical model in Essbase. Both metadata and data can be brought over.

8. Drilling back to any data source associated to studio. This comes in handy when we intend to create data marts from a ROLAP data warehouse and add it as a source to Essbase Studio. This data mart can be associated with metrics for analytics or serve as source for reports by dept or subject area.

This method of segmenting reporting can be done for Analytical BI that involves reporting on a nightly basis. Multiple data marts can be used for drill-through and drill back, depending on the business needs of the data analysis desired.

9. Creating once and using multiple times. Any Essbase cube that has a dimension that is part of the report can gain access to the report. This is because drill-through reports are independent of the deployed model.
10. Using OBIEE as a data source for Essbase to drill back to/from Essbase.
11. Using multidimensional cubes as a data source for reporting and analytics, including forward-looking analytics.
12. Reporting data lineage for a particular element or a model in itself as a chart.
13. Employing smart view to derive Excel- and Office-based data and add extra dimensionality to reporting. The seamless interoperability of Essbase and Excel opens another door to defining and sharing data, analytics, and reports. Also, it is possible to drill-through from data directly from Excel. This extends BI analysis beyond disconnected spreadsheets.

6.3.3 Using ASO Cubes for Analytical BI

Essbase ASO cubes don't require preaggregation in order to see data at the upper levels. Instead, ASO cubes dynamically calculate data to aggregate levels. To reduce query time, values can be preaggregated and stored as aggregate views. Retrievals then start from the closest aggregate view are calculated from there.

Smart lists (Text and Date measures) can be used for Analytical BI.

The Essbase analytics link enables single reporting for custom financial analytics via modified dimensionality, as well as merging of additional data sources. It also allows for real-time or on-demand data synchronization, thereby enabling real-time reporting.

Figure 6.2 gives a high-level overview of using ASO and BSO Cubes for Analytical BI.

Oracle Essbase for analytical revolves around the fact that it provides for modeling of a single platform of all related data via

- The logical (dimensional) model and source-to-target mapping
- Business-to-technology transformation
- Commonality and standardized metadata for Essbase and OBIEE

6.4 Summary

This chapter outlined the use of Essbase for Analytical BI. This is of primary importance in using Essbase for real-world decision making and plays a pivotal role in data integration and analytics for analysis. Starting with the kind of analytics that are suited for Essbase, the chapter highlighted the implementation

High-Level Overview of Using ASO and BSO Cubes for Analytical BI

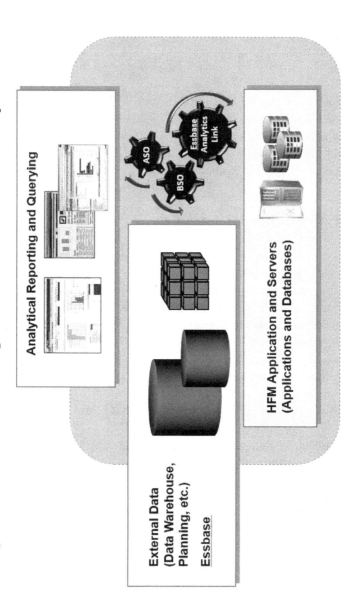

Figure 6.2 High-Level Overview of Using Essbase ASO and BSO Cubes for Analytical BI. (Reproduced with permission from BIS3 LLC © 2015.)

specifics of using Essbase for Analytical BI. The focus of the next chapters will be on OBIEE and using it effectively in the context of Operational BI.

6.5 References

1. "Oracle BI: Business Intelligence." Oracle website: http://www.oracle.com/bi.
2. "Oracle Essbase 11.1.2—Oracle by Example" (tutorials). Oracle website: http://www.oracle.com/technetwork/middleware/essbase/tutorials/ess1112-396125.html.
3. "Essbase Studio 11.1.2 Product Overview." Oracle website: http://www.oracle.com/webfolder/technetwork/tutorials/tutorial/hyp/EssbaseStudio_11.1.2_Overview/LessonIndex.htm.
4. "Oracle Exalytics In-Memory Machine: A Brief Introduction," January 2014. Oracle white paper: http://www.oracle.com/us/solutions/ent-performance-bi/business-intelligence/exalytics-bi-machine/overview/exalytics-introduction-1372418.pdf.
5. "Oracle Business Intelligence Enterprise Edition Samples." Oracle website: http://www.oracle.com/technetwork/middleware/bi-foundation/obiee-samples-167534.html.
6. "Oracle Essbase," Oracle website: http://www.oracle.com/technetwork/middleware/essbase/overview/index.html.

Chapter 7

Using OBIEE for Operational BI

In This Chapter

7.1 Introduction

In celebration of the decades of implementation and delivery experience, we are writing this book and sharing our secrets for success as practitioners in the field. We have been fortunate to have our careers grow alongside the growth of the industry, and we have helped to pioneer the thoughts, ideas, and approaches that have now become best practices. We stand in awe of the successful development of the industry with its many technological advances into areas that were never before achievable, such as real-time or near real-time processing of large amounts of operational data.

But despite the multitude of these innovations and advancements in business intelligence (BI) and analytical solutions, we still continue to encounter basic errors and mistakes repeatedly performed in building or implementing solutions; thus, we still continue to see failures that plague our industry that should not have to be repeated with some knowledge and expertise. For this reason, this book is somewhat being written to gather and reestablish best practices that are known but perhaps not heeded by some practitioners in the field. In addition, we try to provide valuable real-world experiences gained from actual implementation—as opposed to the ever so plentiful "pie-in-the-sky" advice and theories that may not be relevant in real-world environments and situations. It is therefore our goal to provide you with approaches and methods that actually work out in the field and have become best practices, proven and time-tested by successful practitioners.

To begin with this theme of being a successful practitioner, let us observe the following principal covered in earlier chapters of the book; that is (in layman's terms), do not let the tools or technologies dictate how you handle the data or architect the solution. Rather, observe the best practices of data warehousing and business intelligence and then determine the right tools to use in accordance with the functional reporting or analysis categories you are trying to achieve and develop as a solution. We broadly and generally categorize those as Operational Reporting, Operational BI, or traditional Analytical BI.

In this chapter, we will define those categories and then provide some guidance into using Oracle Business Intelligence Enterprise Edition (OBIEE) for Operational BI. But first, let's review the concept of using the right tool for each categorical BI function.

7.2 Don't Let Your Tool Wag Your Data

We use this phrase in a humorous attempt to urge or even warn our customers to use the right tool for the job. Even today out on the field, time and time again, we are seeing tools and technology being used for the wrong functionality or solution, such as:

- Spreadsheets being used as a data store
- Multidimensional cubes being used as a data warehouse

There are various reasons why the wrong tool may be used for a solution. For the former example, with spreadsheets it could be the comfort level and familiarity with using a spreadsheet for data-driven or data-centric tasks. While a spreadsheet is great for presentation and providing limited data storage, it is not the proper tool to use as a data store where it is relied upon as a complete, accurate source of data.

This improper cross-functional use is quite common, especially with tools that have previously provided a certain capability to users. Often, these tools are readily available and user-friendly enough to provide a self-serve or do-it-yourself capability. Empowered by this, users will often gravitate around the tool to get something done and even press the limits and use the tool in areas that it was not intended. This notion is quite admirable, and in some environments and situations may even be "heroic," in that the job gets done. "So then," you ask, "what exactly is the problem with this?"

The problem often lies in the fact that the tool may have served a purpose and been capable for one person or maybe even a single department; however, it may not be strong or advanced enough to be used enterprise-wide by many people and several departments. In information technology (IT), we point the solution out as not being scalable, flexible, extensible, or even manageable. A prevalent example that we often find is when a spreadsheet application is being used as a data store and is then forwarded as a reliable data source, despite the fact that it may contain various questionable flaws in the data, such as having been manually manipulated or even lacking the mechanisms to be properly updated, among other things. When it is allowed to proliferate, the real problem begins as the flawed solution becomes the de facto standard and becomes the source of unreliable, inaccurate reporting and analysis for the organizations—or worse, because of the resources needed to maintain it, the flawed solution becomes the cause of having limited or no source of accurate, complete data.

The other example provided deals with the misuse of multidimensional cubes. In the early days of this industry, there was a great promise of replacing spreadsheets with new technology for reporting and analysis. That technology was the *cube*, a multidimensional structure that processed and stored data for fast retrieval of aggregated data for analysis. It was different from a relational database management system in the way that it stored its data. At that time, it was the hot new technology that promised an effective, efficient way for handling large amounts of data.

Without a doubt, cubes provided great functionality for such things as slicing and dicing and aggregation of data; however, what cubes cannot do that data warehousing can do or at least can handle more appropriately are things such as data cleansing, incremental loads and updates, and change data capture (CDC) and, in general, anything having to do with preparing large amount of historical data.

Keep in mind the ever-changing world of IT. The very nature of technological advances and innovations in IT ensures an endless stream of new tools and technologies, appearing every so often and promising to provide a better way. The first reaction and expectation is that these new tools and technologies replace the "old," which perhaps may be inefficient or said to be archaic. However, more often than not, these "new" tools and technologies really just build on existing best practices and do not necessarily replace them. The need to gravitate toward the new is something that must be approached with caution—especially in light of all the vendors who heavily market their product as the "Holy Grail" for developing the best solution. But remember not to "let your tool wag your data"—don't follow best practices in an attempt to use a certain tool for all your BI and reporting needs and requirements.

So now that we have provided some discussion on using the wrong tool for reporting or analysis, the authors propose to define and establish specific guidelines for the proper use of various tools in the Oracle BI suite. As stated, these guidelines are for practitioners and implementers who want to achieve success in designing and implementing a complete, holistic BI solution that addresses and includes various types and categories of reporting and analytics. In this chapter, the focus is on a specialized type of reporting and business intelligence that actually carries the characteristics of real-time reporting and analysis at the same time. Let us examine the various categories of reporting and analytics and see how Operational Business Intelligence (or Operational BI, as we refer to it for short) fits in the big picture and what it has to offer.

7.3 Categories for Business Intelligence and Reporting

Through the recent decades, reporting and analytics have matured to offer various kinds of capabilities and functionality in decision support. The industry has grown to include innovative and sophisticated methods and approaches for reporting and analysis under what is generally labeled as business intelligence. Indeed, BI has evolved to offer different, various kinds of capabilities and functionalities so much so as to categorize these capabilities into distinct requirements and solutions—each with its own criteria of success, to include such things as proper architecture, infrastructure, or even performance levels.

Although the industry has evolved into distinct categories, today's BI landscape contains complications brought on by the fact that BI has become a catch-all term to describe and include everything that remotely deals with handling data and reporting. As a practitioner and implementer of BI, this is usually the first step to overcome with the intended audience. Education of the users is a key factor of success and acceptance of the solution, as users often do not understand or know the various distinguishing capabilities, characteristics, and components of BI that can make up a complete and holistic solution.

So what are the characteristics of Operational BI? How does it differ from other components of the solution such as reporting? Moreover, in a holistic strategy for reporting and intelligence, how can you recognize and distinguish between what is Operational BI and another closely related system, such as what is commonly known and traditionally viewed as Analytical BI? More importantly, how does each one truly fit into your organization's capability and system for reporting and analytics as a whole?

To answer these inquiries, let's start by recognizing that a general categorization of BI and reporting could be organized and classified into three distinct categories:

- Operational Reporting
- Analytical BI
- Operational BI

To understand these, let us begin by examining the first two: Operational Reporting and Analytical BI. These two represent the extreme left and right of our categories. Taking these characteristics and comparing them side by side, we begin to understand how each category of reporting and analytics would be used to accomplish a particular set of requirements and capabilities. Table 7.1 examines the distinguishing characteristics and compares Operational Reporting to Analytical BI.

Table 7.1 Comparison between Operational Reporting and Analytical BI

	Operational Reporting	Analytical BI
Analytical Capability	n/a	Specifically used for analytics
Latency	Immediate	Commonly a one-day lag, depending on scheduled refresh
Underlying Structure	3rd Normal Form as usually architected for systems for Online Transactional Processing (OLTP)	Multidimensional structure commonly referred to as a cube

After examining the characteristics of these two categories, a third category that involves real-time analytics between these two may be needed to complete your corporate strategy for reporting and analytics. Indeed this categorization "sits" in the middle of these two and "borrows" characteristics and requirements listed for Operational Reporting and Analytical BI to come up with a third categorization of reporting and analytics, which we refer to as Operational BI. Table 7.2 examines Operational BI in relation to Operational Reporting and Analytical BI.

Comparison of Operational BI

Table 7.2 Comparison of Operational BI in Relation to
Operational Reporting and Analytical BI

	Operational Reporting	Operational BI	Analytical BI
Analytical Capability	n/a	Capable	Specifically used for analytics
Latency	Immediate	Usually refreshed daily or can be processed intraday	Commonly a one-day lag depending on scheduled refresh
Underlying Structure	3rd Normal Form as usually architected for systems for Online Transactional Processing (OLTP)	Star Schema or dimensional model as usually architected for decision support systems, such as for Online Analytical Processing (OLAP)	Multidimensional structure commonly referred to as a cube

In adhering to this approach, these three general categorizations can now form the basic guidelines for what a holistic business intelligence solution can and should offer. This chapter specifically looks at Operational BI and the other categories will be discussed separately in respective chapters.

7.4 What Is Operational Business Intelligence?

Tactical decision making (as opposed to strategic) with data coming from the operational or transactional systems of an enterprise form systems used to conduct business on a day-to-day basis. One such enterprise system would be a sales order entry system to input orders from customers for example. Naturally, some form of reporting and intelligence is needed to handle and understand the organization's position and information is basically needed of the sales. So this financial reporting is a great sample of the kind of reporting and intelligence needed by organization and falls under this category of operational business intelligence. Let's further examine the characteristics of Operational BI and how it differs from reporting and traditional Analytical BI.

If we were to look at certain overriding characteristics of Operational BI, it would have to contain faster access to the data and its distribution. This faster access and distribution can be achieved in a much more timely manner than traditional Analytical BI because the mechanism (i.e., the cube) requires additional time to process. The cube requires this process in order to provide for performance in the proper formatting. The various types of overlap may provide the answer to being able to handle your requirements between operational and analytical. We have set forward this theme that OBIEE best serves to satisfy the requirements of Operational BI. So then let us further examine Operational BI.

Operational BI provides users in an organization time-sensitive information or intelligence regarding their operational systems. In regards to this requirement to deliver vital information within hours—or moreover, even minutes—perhaps the biggest challenge for Operational BI is the architecture of the system and addressing the challenges and limitations of near real-time or real-time analysis and reporting often required of this type of solution. This complex requirement alone calls for the right decision from organizations to decide the right architecture and technologies to enable and reap the benefits of what Operational BI can offer.

7.4.1 The Ultimate Goal: Insight to Interaction

The goal that the authors proffer is to create a holistic and complete system for operational business intelligence and analytics to provide the information, knowledge, or intelligence to support decision making related to running the operations of an organization. Moreover, upon receiving this intelligence, the true ultimate goal is to gain insight and some ability to interact and follow through with the insight provided by your system to affect some change to your desired goal. In simpler terms, the goal is to be able to gain some kind of intelligence that can be used to your advantage. In this way, the insight turns into some valuable interaction. After all, what good is the knowledge and intelligence if you can't do anything with it? Let's look at one example of where this intelligence can turn into insight and, moreover, interaction.

7.4.1.1 Sample Operational BI Insights and Interactions

The whole idea of Operational BI then is to be able to gain insight quickly concerning operations and be able to react with an action to take advantage of the insight. After all, what good is data if it doesn't provide any real advantage or result—what you have, in essence, is exactly that; just a bunch of data. So, in other words, the real importance lies in not only being able to provide the right data to the right person at the right time but to also have the right insights and interaction with the data.

Take for instance the example where the transactional system would take an order and in doing so would be able to gauge a corresponding result as to the supply level of materials needed to create that product that was ordered.

So in other words, with this capability, items in inventory can be ordered in advance to manufacture the product. The inventory level of raw materials used and consumed for manufacturing is properly gauged and measured. Through this process operational business intelligence is able to determine that raw materials used in the manufacturing of the product and determine whether materials are running low in supply. So as the order is taken, the system simultaneously reorders more raw material to satisfy any future orders. This is just but one example of how Operational BI could get the right data to the right person at the right time and consequently gain an advantage in keeping the business of manufacturing running smooth by decreasing the chance of running out of material and not lose an opportunity to sell more products due to a shortage of raw material for manufacturing. It may seem very simple but at this time of writing it has taken decades to effectively be able to source data from transactional systems and move and transform it in a way that it is usable for analysis within the course of a day. This time-sensitive capability of business intelligence or analytics of an operational system that can offer a real competitive advantage to any organization is Operational BI.

With this goal in mind, we now turn our focus in this chapter to being able to deliver that system or solution that can provide the necessary operational business intelligence and analytics to achieve the goal previously described. We now reveal the practitioner's secrets necessary to succeed in delivering a holistic and complete solution for Operational BI.

Operational BI for near real-time data analytics and analysis can be centralized around an Operational Data Store (ODS) complementing the EDW that does function as a persistent store of nightly or inter-day data. The ODS can deliver minute-by-minute data from operational systems by way of creation of semantic views based on a logical data model and the data for the views being materialized on the fly. These views eliminate the need to move data physically in addition to giving the flexibility to transform and reload data on the fly. Another approach can be in-memory caching of a table of metrics/KPIs for dashboards in OBIEE. Operational BI can benefit from both of these approaches and deliver near-time data for analytics and analysis.

7.5 Delivering Operational BI

The underlying data structures and data architecture supporting the BI solution are the enablers most often overlooked when developing or implementing a solution entailing Operational BI. For structured data in a corporate environment, proper data modeling is vital in developing an Enterprise Data Warehouse. This is the "secret sauce" that at times, whether because of lack of expertise or even knowledge, is sometimes dismissed and is the cause of much of the failure that plagues the industry. In the past and even with some of today's new tools and technologies, vendors have incorporated strategies and approaches attempting to avoid having to model the data. Although it is perhaps permissible for unstructured data to be in a setting for discovery, not modeling the data in a structured environment and solution such as for an enterprise data warehouse is not good practice. It would be analogous to building a house without a blueprint. Today's best practices for building BI solutions have reached the maturity to fully understand the limitations and capabilities of various different data structures and architectures as they relate to the various different categories and types of BI solution, ranging from Operational BI to Analytical BI and beyond.

In this chapter, we have focused on structured data in a corporate environment to deliver business intelligence and analytics based on operational data and associated business processes. This book doesn't necessarily go into the details of how to create the various structures, as there are many instructional books and writings concerning data architecture and the different types of foundational data structures for creating BI solutions. The basic choices are whether the data is normalized (e.g., to the 3rd Normal Form) or is de-normalized (as in a dimensional model or star schema). Although best practices have now been established through decades of maturity in the industry, it is surprising that debates still linger as to which structure is best to support reporting and analytics. As practitioners with extensive experience and expertise, we have determined through proven practical application which structure and foundation truly support a holistic and complete BI solution. We forward a basic fundamental strategy for BI as it pertains to reporting and analytics. That basic strategy and approach is the dimensional model or star schema, as found in an enterprise data warehouse and corresponding repository utilized in OBIEE.

7.5.1 Operational BI and OBIEE

OBIEE specifically supports and provides for Operational BI through its repository of data logically modeled through its Business Modeling and Mapping (BMM) utility in the BI Server layer. Through a BI Admin tool, the BMM is created in accordance with the physical layer exposed through the tool. The BMM is used to create the dimensional model or star schema and can even utilize data structures that have already been architected dimensionally at the database layer. As a relational online analytical processing (ROLAP) solution, it effectively makes use of the relational database management system (or RDBMS) that stores the data. In supporting the capability of querying and analysis, the data is ideally already architected and structured as dimensional model or star schema. In that case, the logical data model used to create the structures in the database can also be used as a guide for creating the data model and setting up the logical structures of the BMM.

The complications of Operational BI are the underlying added functionality and the requirement to provide trending and historical views of data along with real-time or near real-time data. In essence, this functionality combines the elements of reporting and analysis simultaneously. This unique combination of functionality can confuse practitioners and implementers as to exactly what type of system, and consequently architecture and infrastructure, is needed to deliver this solution and capability to the users. Therefore, to accompany the proper structure and architecture to support the Operational BI solution, the appropriate process also needs to be determined and explored. Essentially, for an Operational BI solution, an efficient, continual process is needed to update the underlying structures (e.g., an enterprise data warehouse, or EDW) with an incremental loading routine of adding new data in the source system to what is already existing and stored in the EDW. This will allow for a streamlined process and approach for accessing the most current data added from the source.

To create historical records and provide for trending analysis utilizing data from the EDW, the following general rules are needed:

- The EDW needs to be *time-variant* (the records should be dependent on a time factor). This can be achieved with a timestamp column, which basically creates a separate record of the same data elements, recorded and tracked through time.
- Changes to pertinent business data need to be examined, and the changes that need to be captured and stored in the EDW must be determined. Examples of changes include changes to an employee's name, customer address, item description, or even a salesperson territory assignment. All these provide information about a certain sale, revenue, or any other factual transaction and can provide valuable insight to the nature of the transaction through time and history. The business user community will need to determine what changes to data should be recorded and stored in the EDW to track historical reporting and trending.

Let's explore how to update the EDW, and later in the chapter, we will explore accessing that new data not from the EDW but from another structure called an Operational Data Store (ODS), which serves as a great source of cleansed data for the EDW—especially new operational data that has been incrementally targeted and captured as real-time or near real-time changes to the source data. You will find that both relational database structures—the EDW and the ODS—can serve as the source of data to Operational BI.

7.5.2 Updating the Enterprise Data Warehouse for Operational BI

In support of Operational BI, it is important to know the various methods for updating the enterprise data warehouse with new or modified records from the source. In general, there are two basic ways to accomplish this. These two methods can be labeled and described as a *complete refresh* and an *incremental update* (see Figure 7.1).

In a complete refresh, the tables in the target are either truncated or over-written in their entirety with the complete set of data existing in the source at the moment. In contrast, an incremental update would look to the source system and perform a comparison to identify any changes in the data. It then appends the existing set of data already in the target tables. In this way, the table is said to be updated incrementally—as opposed to overwriting the data and completely refreshing the database. The following is a very simplistic depiction of the difference in data processing and data flow using a complete refresh versus incremental updates. In a complete refresh, the target tables are completely overwritten in a simple extract, transform, and load (ETL) that processes the data in bulk; for an incremental update, new records identified in the source system are processed specifically for each target with a special ETL to handle each source and target to create new records in the target tables of the data warehouse.

Both methods and approaches are generally permissible, but one may be more appropriate than the other when considering such things as data volume, storage capabilities, or even timeliness of new data.

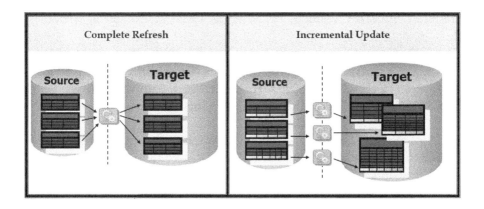

Figure 7.1   Complete Refresh and Incremental Update

7.5.2.1 Considering Requirements for Slowly Changing Dimensions (SCD) Types

It is common for an EDW to be refreshed completely when new data is processed. In other words, only the most current data found in the transactional system is kept and overwrites the data that was previously stored. As such, the EDW does not currently contain any historical records and does not keep any trending information. In developing a star schema for your data mart, this is called an SCD Type 1 as opposed to SCD Type 2 and SCD Type 3, which contain complete history and limited history, respectively.

This book does not go into detail on how to process these slowly changing dimensions, as this subject is well documented. However, let us discuss how to identify the need for historical data and provide some examples. As previously stated the three choices, in respect to history, can be listed as:

- SCD Type 1—no history
- SCD Type 2—complete history
- SCD Type 3—limited history

Each type is pertinent to any organization and the determination must be made as to what kind of historical analysis, if any, is desired. To create the historical records in the EDW, pertinent business data must be identified and deemed as required. Declaring historical records to be included will undoubtedly affect reporting outcomes and results as well as system performance.

In summary, the different methods for handling changes made to the dimensional data in your EDW can be summarized into three distinct categories; business users must determine which of the three is appropriate for capturing history or any changes in the source data to meet their requirement to retain historical records or trending, if any, such as listed in the following section.

7.5.2.2 Considering Requirements for Capturing History or Any Changes in the Source Data To Meet the Requirements To Retain Historical Records or Trending

An incremental daily load can capture historical records and trending data in the EDW for Operational BI (see Table 7.3).

The main goal is to capture and identify records that are new to the source data system and not yet stored in the EDW. One such way is to run a Change Data Capture (CDC) process to compare and capture each new record in the source system and process that record in accordance to the SCD rules used in updating the target table, as described earlier in the chapter. In conjunction with identifying and capturing the changes, there may also be a need to group and aggregate these changes and store them as snapshots. In addition to providing a stored view of the data in a referenced point in time, these snapshots can also be utilized for Operational BI for viewing the most current and recent changes.

Table 7.3 Sample Requirements Associated with Running an Incremental Daily Load To Capture Historical Records and Trending Data in the EDW for Operational BI

Process/Business Requirement	Description of Requirement	Possible Issues
Uniquely identify Fact record (and grain of Subject Area as a whole)	Create an identifier for each record in the Fact table, based on specified, precise data elements that make a record unique (e.g., natural key).	Records in the Fact table cannot be uniquely identified by their natural key for comparison. The natural key of record contains distinct values for each required data element which can identify its uniqueness.
Historical Records	Provide means to report on past information and historical records from the EDW	The current structures for reporting and analytics only support the most current data—overwriting what is stored in the EDW.
Periodic Snapshots	Provide means to readily access and report on a predefined calendar period	The current structures for reporting and analytics do not aggregate any data.

7.5.2.3 Utilizing Snapshot Copies for Operational BI

Periodic snapshots are copies of data in the EDW which represent a how the data and record existed at that point in time. These predefined and stored aggregates can offer the needed comparison of old and new status to quickly enable Operational BI from an EDW. Two main points in utilizing periodic snapshot copies of the data for Operational BI are as follows:

- Records will be compared as prior and current snapshots in the staging table in the database layer.
- Differences will be reported in the presentation layer via OBIEE.

Basic reporting for snapshots will be provided by comparing various snapshots of the same period. This will allow for quick analysis (see Figure 7.2).

Furthermore, when dealing with historical data for Operational BI, it is common to group it in aggregated groups of data based on the calendar, such as weekly, monthly, quarterly, and annual groups. To facilitate access to data

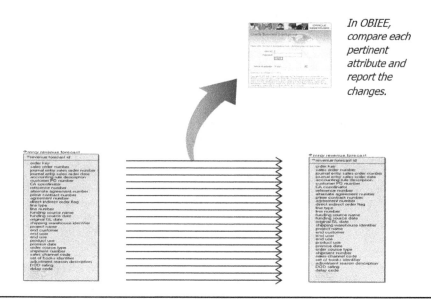

In OBIEE, compare each pertinent attribute and report the changes.

Figure 7.2 Basic Reporting for Snapshots

during these predefined periods, individual aggregates of data called *periodic snapshots* can be stored. The strategy will comprise two components: *incremental updates* to the EDW and *collective snapshots* at each specified period.

Incremental updates at the daily atomic level will be processed. Differences in the record (or data that has changed) will be captured by the ETL logic and added to a single daily (and subsequent other periodical) snapshot at the database layer.

The following is an overview of the steps needed to create snapshot copies of the report and analysis in various subsequent calendar periods.

1. Records are processed daily throughout the week and will be stored as the base table for the analysis and report. This table will contain historical records from the date determined by the business community.
2. At the start of every week, as determined by the business, the latest snapshot is stored to represent the week. This serves as the basic aggregated data which will feed the subsequent snapshots.
3. As data is made available and stored accordingly in the appropriate weekly snapshot, subsequent periods will also be stored accordingly (e.g., month, quarter, and year) per the established schedule for processing. (See Figure 7.3.)

This process is one example of how the underlying structures and related strategies pertaining to the EDW provide quick access to data. In the case of

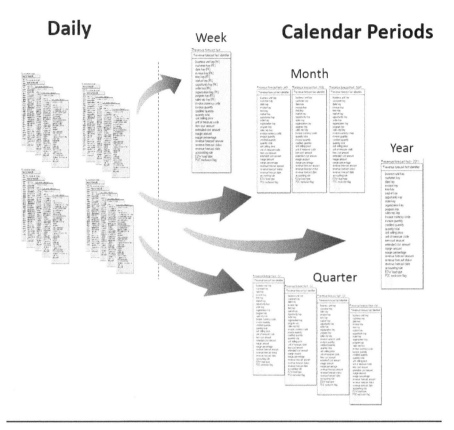

Figure 7.3 Collective Snapshots by Week, Month, Quarter, Year

a well-defined structured data for a given calendar period, such as a week, a month, a quarter, or a year, the EDW can readily store and access the structured data for purposes of using it for Operational BI. The structured data is essentially processed and then stored away for use on demand. In this way, an EDW is the needed enabler to provide Operational BI. However, there is additional option which might be added to the strategy to address the time factor involved when Operational BI needs to be more frequently updated and refreshed nightly or once a day. How can analysis of data intraday or in between the daily refreshes of an EDW be handled? The answer is another enabling structure called an operational data store (ODS).

7.6 The Operational Data Store Option

The EDW is a relational data structure that serves as the data source to Operational BI. The structures are predetermined and properly modeled

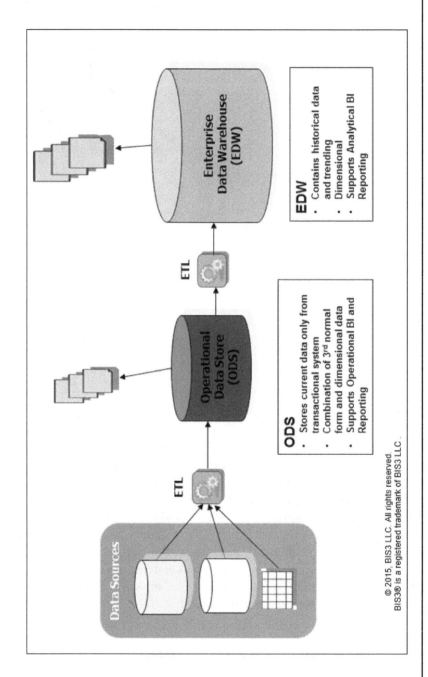

Figure 7.4 Operational Data Store. (Reproduced with permission from BIS3 LLC © 2015.)

dimensionally in a star schema to represent business transactions or facts and related business dimensions that describe the who, what, where, and so forth of that particular subject area. Once the star schema is processed, the data is available for analysis by its consumers for Operational BI. There is no longer a need to process the data again unless, of course, it prepares the data for Analytical BI best served in a cube such as Essbase. In that case, please refer to Chapter 6 of this book.

Although the EDW is the main database structure to serve Operational BI, it may not necessarily meet the requirements for timeliness if the requirement is more frequent than the nightly or once-a-day refresh commonly needed for processing the EDW. In this case, another structure can fill the gap to serve as an intermediary between what can be gathered from the transactional system for reporting and what is currently stored in the EDW for historical analysis and trending. That structure is an ODS (see Figure 7.4).

Essentially, the ODS is refreshed completely when new data is processed. In other words, only the most current data found in the transactional system is kept and the data stored previously in the ODS is overwritten. Processing the ODS changes the content and what is stored. If the ODS is queried, it would only contain the most current data that was processed from the transactional system. It will not contain any historical records or information stored based on the past contents of the EDW.

As a basic strategy for the ODS, the data is refreshed and overwritten each time records from the transactional system are processed. However, in cases where some trending and historical analysis is needed, the ODS can be used to store limited history to meet the requirements of the specific analysis it is trying to obtain. For obvious reasons of maintenance, it should not be another duplicate copy of the EDW.

Because of limitations in the capabilities of tools and technologies, Operational BI was not feasible in the early days of the industry. The processing requirement and preparation of the data for intelligence and analytics simply could not meet the requirements of real-time or near real-time BI. In essence, by the time the right data reached the right person, the intelligence would no longer be fresh or valuable to be fully utilized. In other words, an operational manager or director in charge of such operations would not even have access to the type of information and related insights that would enable them to affect the operational process that could drastically change and even improve business—perhaps even to gain an edge over their competitors. Therefore, the general idea of Operational BI did not even come into play until the tools and technologies enabled for moving data to and from the source to be able to utilize the data, information, and intelligence—and, moreover, the insights that could be potentially gained.

But even before getting to that vital point of gaining insight, the goal of gathering data within an organization or enterprise for use posed a big challenge within itself. For many decades, practitioners struggled as just the mere idea of being able to store all the information together in one place was a big issue. There was simply no easy way of moving large amounts of data to and from one system to another in a timely manner. So during the early days of the Internet, when data suddenly became readily accessible and ubiquitous across the globe, data professionals were searching for methods and approaches that could provide the most effective process for creating intelligence and analytics from raw data. What came of it was the emergence of ETL tools and technologies, and a whole new market was created that readily provided a means to access data that was much needed and desired which in turn fueled the creation of the business intelligence industry.

However, along with the excitement of the new capabilities that it brought, BI hasn't been without its share of complications and user understanding. There has been a lot of confusion about the difference between operational reporting and BI in general. The two subjects are often interchanged and referred to mistakenly. It used to be that reporting only referred to being able to access some data, but it never was meant to gain any kind of insight or analytics based on history. Transactional systems simply did not have the history to begin with. At that time, reporting was really just access to whatever data the transactional system may have had. Any kind of analytics was really formed afterwards with a different system, often through a very manual and labor-intensive process performed by the likes of statisticians and mathematicians. Today's new technologies and tools offer a whole new world of analytics and predictive solutions that now have the capability to distinguish reporting from analytics. However, many users still do not fully understand the purposes and goals for each type of system. This book tries to address and answer that issue.

7.7 Summary

For decision support, the different types of systems that are available for reporting and analytics encompass and are grouped under what is now referred to in general as BI. With advancement of the tools and technologies needed to deliver BI, subcategories emerge or even evolve to form their own set of success criteria and requests. And so it was with Operational BI. In terms of reporting and analytics, a whole new set of criteria and goals have provided a combination of the characteristics of a reporting system and an analytical system. In conjunction with this new set of criteria and goals, it is important to understand that a whole new architecture and approach enables the capability to provide Operational

BI. This chapter provides an overview to this capability and concept which has been successfully addressed with OBIEE.

Different structures and architectures are needed to support various reporting and analytical systems. Not one type of structure can satisfy all requirements at this time. For that reason, it is still common to find some organizations querying a transactional system for analytics (as if it were a decision support system), often with futile results—especially in terms of performance, simply due to the many joins found in a transactional system. In these cases, the short-term vision of being able to access any kind of data from the source system in hopes of gaining some useful information overrides the necessary vision and strategy needed to build a successful holistic, complete BI system and solution. For Operational BI, that holistic and complete solution is supported by the EDW and sometimes the ODS, if needed.

In the future, how great would it be to be able to query any kind of data system without any type of transformations or "heavy-lifting" in order to utilize it for analysis and beyond, such as data mining and predictive analytics? Indeed when technology catches up to where transactional systems and decision support systems use the same structure and architecture in the backend, business intelligence and analytics would take a great leap forward—at the very least, by eliminating additional processing efforts and time needed for transformations and preparations so that efforts could concentrate on what is needed for intelligence and analytics. This approach would truly hit the main goal of getting the right information to the right person at the right time—perhaps within seconds. Imagine the future that that capability would enable.

Chapter 8

Using OBIEE for Self-Service BI

In This Chapter

8.1 Introduction

From the early stages of business intelligence, there have been ample lists of promises and visions of grandeur for what this type of solution can provide for decision makers. In the beginning this reference to decision makers may have been reserved exclusively for executives. That definition and categorization has now been forwarded for all levels of management and decision making and even further to include a broad capability to access and work with data to improve any decision-making process. This capability has been awaited by many practitioners in the hope that BI would be more widely accepted. Because of the new technologies that have come up through the years it has garnered a lot of attention of late for practitioners as one of the functionalities that a business intelligence solution should offer and that vendors and practitioners should absolutely deliver.

Vendors have done well in coming up with tools that could fulfill that promise of providing access to all levels of the corporate ladder. No longer was BI reserved for just executives and for only matters of a strategic nature. Now everyone in the company is in on the game and only one thing stood between accessing a wealth of enterprise data and knowledge and that was "how exactly does one query the data?" Naturally, it caused a lot of angst about being able to use the tool effectively or even easily.

So it began this need for self-service BI. It was exactly that function sought after in a BI system that would allow some degree of independence and capability for a user to be able do their own analysis. I'm sure that almost all would agree that this idea of self-service BI is perhaps the true overall vision and essence of what a business intelligence solution should offer anyway. Indeed, the industry has come a long way to be able to offer all the technologies that enable a person to access and readily use large amounts of data. Even at the time of writing, the industry has introduced new tools and technologies (i.e., big data) to help with that task. These new tools and technologies undoubtedly help with the technical capabilities but is it truly enough to allow for Self-Service BI.

This chapter will examine the capabilities and functionalities of OBIEE for Self-Service BI. In addition, a basic guide has been included to quickly display the basic screens and show OBIEE's user-friendly screens and ease of use for ad hoc querying.

8.2 In Search of Self-Service BI

When I first started in the industry, the mere fact that we connected computers to each other to form a local area network and then go beyond to do a wide area network was perhaps the first step in allowing the sharing of data across the enterprise. Indeed, it was one of the very first things we had to address. But surprisingly, it no longer became an issue, and the ubiquitous Internet changed how applications were built. With that, readily sharing data across networks was no longer such a big problem. Anyone from anywhere can now access resources via the Internet, and the user community can now utilize servers and resources from far away. Once very elusive, these advances in technology and tools enable us to now utilize data systems to help ourselves.

Many businesses and business processes relied on experience and even on gut feeling to be able to make decisions. But now, with modern-day business intelligence solutions and systems, not only can decisions be made and supported by factual data but also decisions can be attempted that predict the future.

So when we talk about self-service business intelligence, we have to look at the fact that although the resources and data are accessible, it doesn't necessarily mean that great insights and predictive analytics can be made despite the advancements in technology and tools. So what is truly meant by self-service? The elements of the solution would have to address the following:

- ○ Access to pertinent data
- ○ Performance and processing power
- ○ Friendly user interface
- ○ Ability to readily add and append pieces of new data
- ○ Visualization of the data to make insights

With these, an organization could really provide the necessary capabilities for data analysis in the hope that some kind of insight could be gained from data sources that would otherwise be useless and provide no advantage to that organization.

But even with these advancements in technology and tools, can a user truly utilize these systems and solutions? After all, it is not merely about the data. Along with it, there must be some kind of understanding of the business first in order to really form business insights from raw data. Otherwise, how would you know what kind of target or analysis is pertinent and being asked of the raw data? How would you also know how to put certain pieces of data together to form some kind of useful intelligence? The most sophisticated system and solution created would be rather useless in those cases where an understanding of business is not applied. So even gauging the effectiveness of the business solution as being "self-service" would be rather misleading, or even elusive. In other words, the great promise of self-service business intelligence would not be satisfied, but it is only because of the limitations of the person's understanding, not the limitations of the system solution that is provided. So with a plethora of tools and technologies in today's BI landscape claiming ease of use, there are now numerous claims of platforms offering self-service BI.

8.3 Enter OBIEE as a Solution

Access to data in a database for the normal person is difficult, as the normal person doesn't necessarily understand why tables and columns exist. It is because of this that vendors have attempted to come up with an easy way to access data and to analyze data from a database. OBIEE has a tool called Analysis (previously named Answers) in which users with the drop of a column could come up with answers—no pun intended—to their inquiries.

Easily sectioned as tabs, OBIEE Analysis allows a person to pick certain columns from a table and drop them into a design board, so that the person may then easily view the results tab to display the results of their query. The simplicity of design allows the average person to access the data without having to write an SQL file script. To the average user, this is light years ahead. If needed, advanced users can go beyond the simple dropping of columns and selection of columns, and go into writing complex formulas by using the formula button.

The overall idea is to have a selection of attributes for your query and then to filter out certain pieces of data. This will be demonstrated in the next section as we guide you through creating your first Analysis.

Also offered, but in a limited functionality, is a way to format and create a report from your results. The limitations of the tool are only due to the fact that is it is browser-based. However, this is also one of its strengths, in that no special client is needed to be installed. So if you know how to move around a web page in a browser, you can move easily through the OBIEE screen page.

This setup of selecting and dropping columns and attributes into one page and then providing conditions and filters to the data for the side result is the strength of OBI. This tool is the closest to having a self-service solution and system for business intelligence; a normal worker can maneuver in and around the system to readily access and utilize data for information knowledge and intelligence.

But this is only the user interface; what is more important is that the foundation behind it is in order to provide for good clean data. The structure of the data should be emphasized because normal users should be able to see their business, to view the mentions readily and visibly, and to see and understand the structure. For instance, if they want customer information, they should be able to view all the attributes of that particular entity such as "First Name," "Last Name," etc.

As Ralph Kimball, a pioneer in data warehousing and business intelligence, wrote in his industry ground-breaking book *The Data Warehouse Toolkit* for business intelligence practitioners, there were two reasons why a star schema might be needed for decision-support. One reason was particularly for the technical aspect for performance—data fashioned in the star will perform much better in a relational database management system (RDBMS) than in a 3rd normal form structure for a transactional system. This fact must be emphasized and yielded to because many people actually encounter problems when they try to create a query and transaction, and the closest support system is based off of transactional structure in the background. This book doesn't go into the details of the Kimball approach and dimensions modeling except to say that when the data is structured in a star schema it consist of dimensions and facts. Structured correctly, the technical aspects for performance are then successfully addressed and thus set up the second prong and reason for designing and modeling the data dimensionally in a star schema.

The second prong of the Kimball approach deals with what he referred to as "User Understandability." In other words, the data should be presented in a way that can be easily translated and understood by business users. In very basic terms, business data can be categorized under two types of entities: a dimension or a fact. Data that is transactional in nature and can serve as measurements and metrics are called *facts*. To complement and describe those facts, the *dimensions* contain the fields that serve as descriptors. The descriptors are attributes that describe *who*, *what*, *when*, and *where*, among other things. By selecting descriptors, a user can select a record that describes sales, for instance; then the user can select an attribute, such as who bought the product, what the product is, when the product was sold, or how much the product was sold for. As a result, the business user can easily see and analyze the sales to find the who, what, where, and when of that sale.

With the data architecture established, we now turn to the front-end tool that should allow a business user to readily query and analyze the data: Enter Oracle's OBIEE.

8.4 OBIEE for Self-Service BI

As advocates for using OBIEE as a tool for Self-Service BI, we highlight its ease of use for creating a simple analysis of data without having to know a programming or querying language typically used to extract data from a database. The tool has a number of options for creating an analysis, including an option for a direct database request for advanced users. This speaks to the strength of OBIEE; however, we will not focus on that particular piece here.

Rather, the basic mechanism for creating an analysis is the design board, which begins with a blank view—analogous to a blank slate of paper. This is where it all begins. With an idea or query in mind, OBIEE is used for ad hoc or on-demand report reporting, readily satisfying the sought-after self-service capability. This basic and simple method for query and analysis is represented by two tabs, *Criteria* and *Results*, that are used to toggle between selecting data elements (drag and drop) as criteria and then easily viewing the results or values of the data elements that were selected. It is that simple.

As a precursor to this self-service capability, a subject area is prepared in which the data is grouped together in a logical model or categories representing the data readily understood by the user. We've previously discussed and described this logical model from a technical standpoint as a dimensional model or star schema consisting of metrics and measurements and descriptors as dimensions to answer what we refer to as the Who, What, and Where about the metric and measurement.

With this proper data foundation and groupings into subject areas, the data elements are contained and can be found under the respective subject areas folders. For an analysis about the subject area, simply locate the columns for your analysis, choosing as many attributes as needed or desired. Keep in mind that too many options might yield a large table of results, so it is good practice to start with only a few. Simply click and hold to drag and drop the field into the design pane. Organize and reorganize the selected data elements by clicking and dragging them where you would like them. The order of the attributes affects how the analysis will display and look. With all the columns from the tables ordered accordingly, the analysis can be previewed readily by clicking on the *Results* tab. The result is a table that contains the value of all the data elements that were previously added when selected in Criteria.

The basic operation of selecting data elements in the *Criteria* tab and then viewing the resulting data set in the *Results* tab is the simple—yet powerful—method for querying the database. It is important to note that no code or script is needed to view the data. Moreover, this ad hoc function and capability is performed "on the fly" against the subject area in the data warehouse. As such, the resulting data set is not hard-coded, nor is it static. The data result will change dynamically in accordance to the criteria selections and will yield different results as the data in the data warehouse is updated.

This ability to readily access your data with a user-friendly application is the power provided by OBIEE to its users. Armed with knowledge of the data and subject area, this mechanism provided by OBIEE for ad hoc querying of the enterprise data warehouse can confidently be provided and utilized by everyone in your organization, and therefore it can accurately be classified as self-service.

Moreover, recent additions, prompted by changes and demands from the industry for self-service, have pushed OBIEE capabilities, enabling the linking of external data (such as data from a spreadsheet) to append and enhance the data already contained and prepared in the data warehouse. Recent advancements have allowed this to be done dynamically, "on the fly." No longer does the data warehouse sit in a vacuum, dependent on a rigorous and laborious mechanism for effective utilization as a valuable asset for data discovery and predictive analytics. Indeed, advances like these that allow for data mashups and data visualizations have spurred another growth in BI into the realm of advanced analytics and effective data mining under what is now generally being called *data science*.

For this new capability of BI and data science, effective tools are needed for the users and practitioners who warrant access to voluminous amounts of various types of data—and lots of it, coming in as fast as thought. The industry is in need of being able to gather, transform, and maintain this data while at the same time enabling users (or even data scientists) to easily and powerfully serve up and query the data themselves in a self-service capacity. We proffer that the Self-Service BI tool that the industry has been searching for, the one that can integrate an established enterprise data warehouse with pieces of external data for data discovery, is now here. That Self-Service BI tool is OBIEE.

8.5 Big Data and Self-Service BI

Self-Service BI revolves around the fact that decision making using data is aided in particular by interactive and (business-)user driven interfaces to the underlying data. Data today consists not only of structured but also of unstructured data (the so-called Big Data) characterized by volume, velocity, and variety. This data demands fast processing as well as an integrated approach to the analysis of online transaction processing (OLTP) and online analytical processing (OLAP) data and the discovery of new information from that data.

As a result, Big Data for decision making must support new data, new analytics, and new metrics that involve past performance analytics (such as last week's data) along with predictive analytics to ascertain what might happen and model development.

The common dynamic for all of this is self-service, with such analytics depending on what is being asked for and who is being asked for. The agile and changing needs of business users fit perfectly into this dynamic. When it comes to Oracle BI, Oracle Big Data and Oracle Data Discovery provide

- *Real-time analytics of data, self-service analytics to all types of data, and scale-out adoption of the same with interactive data visualization as a major component of the same*
- *Access to relevant and right-time data and self-service access to that data. This means such data can be contextualized within the business process domain of the user asking for and accessing the data*
- *Data that is secure, complete, and granular*

When self-service analytics become a reality made possible by such technologies, business analysis processes such as mobile device management (MDX), visual discovery, and spreadsheet analysis become (business-)user driven, with no disconnect across all needed data points.

Just as OBIEE combined with Oracle Essbase provides a holistic solution to enable predictive analytics and operational and self-service reporting on structured data, Oracle Big Data Discovery can enable extending BI beyond relational data and its multidimensional analysis, which in turn allows self-service analytics on Big Data. This can answer the what, who, why, how of Big Data in near real-time and in a future-oriented fashion.

8.5.1 OBIEE12c and Big Data

As a new wave of analysis and intelligence, BI and Big Data analytics factors into mainstream adoption and self-service analytics on all data that enables near real-time decision making is what is trending now. *OBIEE12c and Oracle Cloud* solutions now enable "self-service" analytics and big data and go the extra mile in facilitating and effecting the change of the status quo. Be it data classified under the Vs sourced from clickstream data warehousing and web log analysis or the billions of transactional rows coming from OLTP, the quick and meaningful handling of such data, turning it into insight in near real-time, always remains the business goal. Oracle has evolved into the Big Data realm with Oracle Exadata and Exalytics at the back end and OBIEE 12c on the front end to be the leader in the BI of the future realm.

Oracle 12c and OBIEE12c support the three major requirements of Big Data Analytics in general and Self-Service Analytics in particular, namely:

1. *Multi-tenancy—The new cloud style infrastructure, multi-service instance (MSI)–enabled*
2. *In-memory optimizations—Oracle Exalytics and implicit columnar technology*
3. *In-memory analytics and advanced analytics*
4. *Data discovery*
5. *Data mash-ups at run-time*
6. *Multidimensional analysis using embedded Essbase engine based on (logical) dimensional model in OBIEE12c*
7. *Pluggable BI—One OBIEE 12c engine servicing multiple BI applications*
8. *Data visualizations at run-time—Self-service analytics and new data science techniques*
9. *Data science*
10. *Cloud*

OBIEE12c offers self-service analytics by providing users the autonomy to analyze and provide analysis based on their own data at run-time. As a result, users have the ad hoc capability to bring in big data from various types of resources and "mash" it up with enterprise data. These are advantages to the user base in terms of user preference and intuitiveness, as well as analysis, intelligence, and analytics. Though this requires the users to master some skills (and, therefore, for administrators to provide certain training and resources), the business benefits derived from such a holistic Big Data BI solution far outweigh these considerations. From technical standpoint, Oracle now supports the hardware and infrastructure to run a resource intensive data driven BI and Analytics application on the front end by way of its Exadata and Exalytics solution offerings, with OBIEE12c complementing the front end part of it.

8.6 Summary

This chapter should provide a clear example and view of the capabilities of Oracle BI and how it can easily serve the standard need for ad hoc reporting and research capabilities. The intention was to show how easily it can be used as a self-service BI tool. In the past, there was no easy way to access data without a certain degree of knowledge and understanding of the technical aspects needed for querying the database. What Oracle has achieved is a simple drag-and-drop interface that enables any user to query stored data. We feel that this process is efficient enough to be labeled as self-service although we do agree that there is some knowledge and understanding of the subject area being used is necessary. Without the business knowledge behind each data element, the user would not be able to perceive whether the tool is working well and whether or not it is advantageous.

This is a common perception if the goal is not met. Often, what can be easily remedied is seen as extremely problematic, when it actually comes down to being able to pinpoint the issue. Not one tool will solve your problem if you don't understand the business behind the metric measurement that you are going after. To offset this possibility, it is important from the very beginning to gain cooperation and collaboration with business users.

Lastly, this chapter touched upon the concepts of Big Data and Self-Service BI. Mainly, new requirements in advanced analytics as well as data discovery aspects come into play as we step into an era where legions of data scientists, armed with their self-service tool in OBIEE, seek to include external data (or even Big Data) to readily append and enhance the established data warehouse in search of answers to their queries and analysis.

The next chapter focuses on solution implementation and customization and our vital best practice component.

Chapter 9

Best Practices for Solution Implementation and Customization

In This Chapter

- 9.1 Introduction
- 9.2 Establishing a Data Foundation Based on a Logical Model
- 9.3 Extending the Logical Data Model for Implementation and Customization
- 9.4 The Logical Model as a Scalable Best Practice Solution
- 9.5 Summary

9.1 Introduction

Throughout this book, the focus has been on best practices for implementing a successful business intelligence and analytic solution marked by manageability, flexibility, extendibility, scalability, and the like, and accommodating any customizations. Overall, this proven best practice we refer to is to establish a firm foundation for the data which correctly translates and encapsulates the data elements and requirements of the business to enable business intelligence and analytics. This data foundation is called a dimensional model or star schema, and the data architecture forms the basis for any downstream applications, such as decision support systems (e.g., OBIEE) and analytics (e.g., Essbase).

From a technical standpoint, the "translation" of the data occurs via a data model with two major data groupings. Essentially, the data model captures the metrics and measurements needed for analysis by declaring a *fact table*, and the various descriptors and criteria pertaining to the metrics and measurement by declaring the *dimensions* (as they are referred to in dimensional modeling). Practicing data modelers and architects recognize this as a *star schema*. Essentially, this star schema provides the necessary architecture for performance; moreover, it designs and fashions the data in a way that is understandable to business users by incorporating business groupings that are well defined and understood.

To capture and develop the correct dimensional model, the approach used is to create a logical data model. As its name suggests, this models the data in a logical fashion as it pertains to business requirements. This logical data model may stem first from a conceptual model with the main goal of capturing business requirements before committing to any physical data model or even actual coding. In this way, the data architecture and foundation are modeled and the solution can be properly planned.

This chapter explores this vital and crucial best practice for a successful solution implementation and customization.

9.2 Establishing a Data Foundation Based on a Logical Model

The best practice for implementing a holistic solution centers around an underlying data foundation based on a logical model of business objects. This model consists of:

- Related logical objects, both structured and unstructured, at the enclosing top level.
- Establishing modeled entities and their attributes.
- Business Intelligence (BI) data stores—both analytical and operational. The relational online analytical processing (ROLAP) solution can be viewed as virtually the same as multidimensional online analytical processing (MOLAP). The physical implementation can be done using logical objects modeled per business requirements and additionally can include any related big data objects.
- Data discovery, consisting of big data elements; it may be mostly unstructured but can also involve structured objects.
- Data Integration layer that ties together all data sources, including Big Data if related and pertinent (see Figure 9.1).

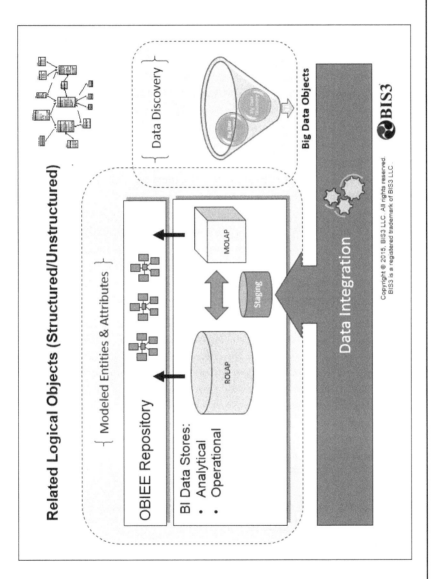

Figure 9.1 One Data Foundation and associated Logical Model. (Reproduced with permission from BIS3 LLC © 2015.)

The logical model is the focus, and it is vitally important in planning out and strategizing the data foundation from a high level. In creating the logical model, the physical implementation is downplayed so as to not dismiss this crucial stage of planning and representing the exact business data objects required to form the data foundation for the enterprise. How this overall data foundation is patterned on an established associated logical model is depicted in Figure 9.1.

Essentially, the established data foundation defines one logical layer that will populate and "feed" both analytical BI and operational BI tools downstream. This logical data foundation can also be extended by a data lake tied to and filtered by data discovery, such as like Oracle Big Data Discovery, Microsoft PowerBI, Tableau, Qlikview, or any other visualization tool in the market.

For implementing Oracle BI and factoring in OBIEE in as part of the solution, the logical (dimensional) model becomes the common information model, encompassing the metadata and semantic layer that is architected and housed in the Repository file or RPD through the Business Modeling and Mapping (BMM) section of the OBIEE Admin tool.

With the common information model established as the data foundation, it can be leveraged and readily utilized to architect and build the Essbase cubes. The remainder of this chapter touches upon how the data is logically modeled and, with the enterprise data warehouse, builds and populates the cubes. It also highlights, as a best practice, how to extend Essbase based on the logical dimensional model to address predictive and prescriptive analytics.

> *We reiterate the way that the data is logically modeled and an enterprise data warehouse is created to feed the cubes. The ROLAP star schema in a relational database management system (RDBMS) is equivalent to the dimensional model in Essbase. As part of best practices for analytics, Oracle Essbase for analytical BI provides for modeling of a single platform of all related data via the logical (dimensional) model and source-to-target mapping, business-to-technology transformation, commonality, and standardized metadata for Essbase and OBIEE.*

9.3 Extending the Logical Data Model for Implementation and Customization

This section gives a detailed explanation of how to extend Essbase so that the ROLAP-based enterprise data warehouse (EDW) can be used to feed the Essbase cubes.

To recap, we begin with reiterating that the Oracle BI Suite, consisting of BI Publisher, OBIEE, and Essbase, constitutes a toolset for holistic BI and analytics. Using BI Publisher for ad hoc (operational) reporting, OBIEE for operational BI, and Essbase for multidimensional analysis and analytical BI provides for a custom implementation of the solution. The tight integration between Essbase and OBIEE enables transparent integration between the two, thus enabling extension of Essbase cubes to create a BI solution that is flexible, extendable, scalable, and manageable.

9.3.1 Using the Logical Model To Extend Essbase Cubes

This is useful for customization of applications that use Essbase for analysis/ analytics. This can be done by using the cube itself or using a star schema in an RDBMS (which subsequently is leveraged to feed the cube).

> *We stress that the star schema created in the RDBMS is essentially the logical equivalent to the dimensional model in Essbase in that both specify and define relevant dimensions associated to target metrics and measurements. The difference lies in the physical implementation of the analytical solution as a ROLAP or MOLAP.*

We recommend the following two methods to extend Essbase based on a logical model:

1. Use the cube as a data mart and as a dimensional model specifying dimensions and their measures.
2. Use a ROLAP star schema in an RDBMS, more specifically sourced from an EDW, as the dimensional model to use for BI and analytics.

The best practical methods to accomplish this are

- In either case, we need to go through the process of putting together a dimensional model that mirrors business requirements (at least on paper). This must involve business users and IT sitting across the board from each other to chalk out specific business requirements, which will be mapped to equivalent technical steps for the dimensional model. This is needed to translate the star to the end user requirements.
- The best practical way to a holistic solution is to architect an EDW based on online transaction processing (OLTP) requirements and have Essbase source data directly from the EDW via XOLAP or using ROLAP star. This allows for performing operational reporting/publishing, analytical BI and operational BI.

- Option 1 from the previous list can be used if there is a unique need to cater to a department that needs to perform MOLAP/analytics and not just flat reporting. XOLAP can be used to directly and transparently source the data from OLTP/RDBMS and feed the cube via the dimensional model in Essbase Studio.
- Option 2 can be used if there is a need for both reporting as well as analytics. In this case, the ROLAP star can subsequently be leveraged and used to feed the cube via the logical dimensional model in Essbase Studio.

The steps involving in building a cube in Essbase Studio based on a ROLAP star that is based on the logical dimensional model are as follows:

1. Design a ROLAP model (star schema).
2. Design a data connection based on this ROLAP model.
3. Design an Essbase cube based on the ROLAP star created in step 1. This way, the ROLAP feeds the data to the cube.
4. Repeat step 3 for any similar cubes that need to be designed based on members of the Essbase outline or any additional dimensions/measures from the ROLAP model.
5. Design an Essbase model based on this cube.
6. Deploy the cube.

> *Recommendation: These two options as explained above can be used to extend the existing cubes, build additional cubes, or perform analytics.*

Essbase can be extended and analytics can be applied to custom implementations (see Figure 9.2).

9.3.2 Building Analytics That Can Be Applied to Custom Implementations

A ROLAP dimensional model as outlined in the previous subsection for extending Essbase Cubes can also be used to perform analytics as needed.

The authors emphasize the following best practices for applying analytics to custom Essbase Implementations:

1. *Perform hybrid OLTP/OLAP analytics*—Start with a ROLAP dimensional model to represent particular business processes that need the final analytics as actionable insights. This leads to an integrated approach by which we analyze ad hoc reporting (BI Publisher), operational BI

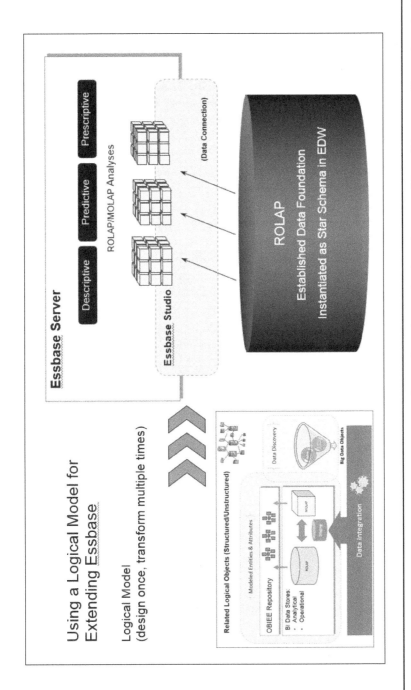

Figure 9.2 Using a Logical Model to Extend Essbase for Analytical BI, Hybrid Analytics, and Data Discovery. (Reproduced with permission from BIS3 LLC © 2015.)

(OBIEE) using ROLAP through a star schema, and multidimensional analysis (in Essbase) for MOLAP/analytical BI. This is the right foundation that gives a holistic solution.

Create the dimensional logical ROLAP model outside of Essbase Studio. This is a better way. As a first exercise, this can be done as a prototype in Essbase Studio and then formally industrialized outside Essbase Studio. This is a fantastic process that enables a connection straight to transactional OLTP systems and also uses analytical data to conduct hybrid analytics.

---

2. *Perform descriptive, predictive, and prescriptive analytics*—As an extension of the first step in this list, customizing Essbase via ROLAP models and integrating these models into Essbase enables the simultaneous performance of BI and Advanced analytics. This means performing *descriptive analytics on data from transactional (OLTP) systems and predictive analytics (what now and what if)* from both OLTP and OLAP systems with subsecond response times. The latter can be done using Essbase BSO cubes. The former can be done using ASO cubes that are efficient and scalable across thousands of concurrent users. The outcomes from predictive analytics can be enhanced to derive *prescriptive analytics (what next)* that provide recommendations for actionable decision making. Predictive analytics can be done in the following manner:
   - Define dimension hierarchies corresponding to business structures such as business dimensions. This can be standardized as "scenario" dimensions.
   - Based on *what now* (e.g., trending and similar occurrences), derive *what if* rules that can be ranked based on likelihood and closeness to the business process involved.
   - Create data that models the *what if* scenarios and outcomes that align with *what next*.
   - Try and incorporate the predictive model as a standard business process using the multiuser read/write capabilities and write-back feature of Essbase.

9.3.3 Best Practices and Additional Customization Scenarios

This section outlines some best practices and additional customization scenarios of using Essbase in the enterprise.

- The Data Integration layer defined in Figure 9.1 can be implemented by leveraging Essbase Studio's functionality based on data source changes.

Essbase Studio supports sourcing from a data warehouse (in ROLAP form) and populating the Essbase cube. Alternatively, a part of the data warehouse can be used as data mart to source the Essbase cube. This takes care of manageability, scalability, flexibility, and extensibility in regard to sourcing data and stuffing the Essbase cube, due to the relational structure of the data warehouse. The warehouse also enables change data capture and incremental data loads.

> *Facts and dimensions required can be modeled in the data warehouse for data aggregations, and any other analyses can be defined and redefined based on current and future requirements, thus making the data integration process change-proof and part of the holistic Essbase and OBIEE solution.*

- Taking into consideration that data is vital to a holistic solution, we assert that all data needs to be validated at the time of sourcing it from point of view of data veracity, integrity, and quality. The following steps need to be performed at the data warehouse layer based on the logical model. There are two aspects in which data can be used for best results:
  - Use load first and then check and transform
  - Use data validation as part of the workflow in the data warehouse; this not only will ensure that data is fully validated during sourcing, but also will allow for a consistent set of pertinent data for the cause for which it is used. This enables to filter data that won't be loaded. Automating this process removes the complexities involved in the process.
  Bad data can be eliminated by checking to ensure that:
  - The data source and data process are consistent.
  - Exceptions have been taken care of.
  - Data is completely validated to its source.
  - Data is completely validated for dimensions and facts.
  - The automated workflow is functioning without any errors or data spills that are outliers.
- Essbase enables a single analytic platform that integrates heterogenous information for yielding insightful business decisions. Essbase Studio, when used at the data source level, enables construction of Essbase cubes based on this platform leveraging a MOLAP data model to push analytics needed. This provides for near real–time (in fact right time) decision making either by using Essbase on its own or by integrating it with Oracle BI.
- XOLAP-based cubes can be implemented in Oracle Essbase Studio to convert Essbase BSO cubes to Hybrid and use them in Hyperion applications for Hybrid and Advanced Relational Access. This in a way optimizes Essbase for Hybrid Analyses. Additionally, BSO's Hybrid ASO-like aggregation can be used. For example, the Hybrid Engine can be used for

cross dimensional hybrid formulas and Hyperion Planning Applications for gathering real-time insight from data.

- SQL-based Essbase integration can help source data from any data source and integrate data and metadata into Essbase more easily and efficiently. SQL queries can be used to load data into Essbase outlines. This process can also be automated in Essbase Studio.
- Use Data Relationship Governance (DRG) within Data Relation Management (DRM) to facilitate the creation and maintenance of master data. Workflow models, requests, governance work lists, alerts and notifications, and paths can be configured right out of the box within DRM. Using runtime substitution variable calculations for allocations across BSO and ASO cubes can be done to make them work together. The corresponding metadata can be synchronized using DRM. Using DRG in a way extends Essbase beyond its normal functionality for governance workflow and approval process by allowing copying of workflow models and tasks, automatic updates for request items, governance Web Service API, database integration, EPM integration, and external workflow.
- Using Essbase in the Cloud enables the creation of ad hoc grids for enterprise financial users and the saving of these grids as reports. The same can be done on premise, too.

9.4 The Logical Model as a Scalable Best Practice Solution

We've described throughout the book the need to establish a firm data foundation to support the downstream applications such as BI and Analytics. The supporting structure is a structured data model instantiated and materialized as an enterprise data warehouse. The enterprise data warehouse is a ROLAP solution created in an RDBMS. If needed, a corresponding MOLAP solution housed in a multidimensional cube can also be used. The best practice for implementing the solution is to model the data logically first. This exercise ensures that the data foundation is well planned and utilized as the enabler and for the overall strategy for the solution. By logically modeling the solution first, no code or effort to build are committed before a design phase is completed. The basic concept is to create the blueprint and roadmap for a successful delivery.

The logical data model also plays a role in Big Data Analytics and Data discovery. The discussion of how this can be done will be presented in the authors' blog at www.essbasestudio.com.

We have established the best practice for dealing with structured data to be used in the enterprise. The architect and creators of the relational database based its concept of handling and relating data on set theory in which the determined sets were made up of members and elements. Determining proper sets and groupings can be a daunting task. As mentioned earlier, this exercise of logically modeling the data is the key to success—a well-proven, time-tested best practice. However, in terms of the unstructured data coming from big data, how does this best practice play out in this new situation and environment? Indeed, the issue becomes one of dealing with integration with the structured data.

The answer still lies with a logical model. The data, whether structured or unstructured, can be examined and assessed as to how a specified object or entity relates to one another. Beginning with the predetermined collection of objects housed in the enterprise data warehouse, a link or relationship can be made to the unstructured data that is discovered. These matching objects are logically related. Once determined, the logically related objects can then be incorporated into the solution. As new tools and technologies emerge in this new arena of structured and unstructured data, we will begin to establish the proper method for modeling these logically related objects and evolve into the next generation of best practices for creating a complete, holistic solution.

9.5 Summary

This chapter described some of the best practices for a holistic BI solution. Starting with explanation of a One Data Foundation and the associated Logical Dimensional Model, it discussed how this logical model can be used to extend Essbase for custom implementations and analytics. Finally, it highlighted using a logical model a best-practice scalable solution. The next chapter deals with industry use cases involving a holistic BI solution based on Oracle Essbase and OBIEE.

Chapter 10

Use Case Scenarios

In This Chapter

10.1 Introduction

The Business Intelligence (BI) industry has grown to now include many vendors offering their products to accomplish their goals of business intelligence and analytics. In very basic terms, that goal can be defined as getting the right data to the right person at the right time. Undoubtedly, all vendors will make the generic claim that their product is the best. But after further analysis and examination of the exact reporting function or analytic capability that is required, it becomes apparent that certain tools and technologies are better suited than others. The true evaluation is not so much about which tools provide BI or analytics but rather which tool is the best fit to the requirement. To make that determination, it helps to understand how the BI space has evolved.

Many early adopters of this concept tried to offer complete suites that went beyond the usual reporting tools and technologies. Early reporting tools struggled with providing analytical capabilities. For that reason, what we saw at that time was a race to develop new technologies, such as multidimensional cubes that promised to deliver solutions enabling the analysis of large amounts of data that were previously unmanageable. The complexity of handling what were then called very large databases (VLDBs) was posing a great challenge, given the sheer volume of data and the complexity of processing the queries that were needed for true analysis. The early adopters and vendors of BI rose to the occasion and through several decades have developed the tools and technologies that now enable business users and consumers to utilize and take advantage of their data beyond simple reporting; now data can supplement good decision making or even help a company gain a competitive edge over the competition. In time, these independent companies and their products became successful in their offerings. As leading-edge corporations adopted the concept of BI and analytics and successfully implemented it, the BI vendors with their product offerings soon caught the eye of major companies looking to get into the game.

So it came to be that the success of the independent BI vendors and their offerings soon became the targets of acquisition for major players who wanted either to kickstart another line of business or to round out their own offerings. Various tracks and paths were taken by big companies, whether through organic growth or acquisition, to offer a complete suite of BI tools and technologies to consumers. The suite of tools provided businesses with the means to establish a foundation for developing and building an enterprise BI solution. As they gained a foot in the door, these companies continued to build their suite of tools and offerings to go beyond the basics of BI to new areas, such as predictive analytics or even artificial intelligence and machine learning. This initial push by the big companies brought BI and analytical tools and technologies to the mainstream. Consequently, it opened up the business world to readily use and trust the concept and strategy for better analytics. As such, BI was here to stay.

But if the BI industry began as a complete holistic solution offered by small, focused vendors, it soon began to be disjointed from the many acquisitions and attempts of the big companies to create seamless and unified product offerings. Often, the proffered unified product was actually made up of several of the previously acquired companies' disparate products with different histories of growth and adoption by the business world. Additionally, to complicate matters, these independent BI companies had different cultures and fostered different kinds of loyalty with their users. Thus, companies inherently preferred to utilize the tool and technology of familiarity, as opposed to utilizing the best fit.

10.2 The Challenge

In earlier chapters, it was suggested that specific tools and technologies match certain features and purposes for reporting and analytics. This seems like a very simple notion, but undoubtedly it is a common occurrence for certain products to be successfully marketed and identified as leading tools for something other than they were intended to be. As such, these products end up "stretched to the limit" to accomplish tasks that were actually better suited for other tools. The primary challenge that is encountered in the BI world is its plethora of vendors, all claiming to be the best tool. Further complicating this issue are the loyal users of the familiar tool, who do not know that other tools may actually better accomplish a certain functionality, or even worse, preferring to use the original tool, ignoring best fit. As the old quip says, "When you have a hammer, everything is a nail."

Such is the issue with Essbase or cubes being used in a data warehousing capacity or the main data repository of data used for decision making. With its popularity in particular to the financial world, it is quite common to see Essbase being used for BI. But BI covers a wide range and area that includes data warehousing, data integration, data visualization, analytics, and the like, all of which come together to form a complete solution. In that context, an Essbase cube would fit into the latter categories for data visualization and analytics but not to serve as a data warehouse and data integration tool. However, we have walked into situations with customers who have used Essbase and cubes in general as the data warehouse or central data repository in support of their holistic enterprise BI and analytics effort.

The issue was that the business users were using cubes to store the data as if they were a processed data mart and the trusted source of data, although the data had been manipulated "by hand" many times, without any necessary controls to ensure its quality. The intention may have started off as a data warehousing effort, but due to misinformation or misguidance of the tools' true capabilities, the solution that resulted was to import data using a cube that could serve as a base and that was, thereafter, daily refreshed and updated with new records to provide the reports or analyses that were requested. Of course this workaround allowed for an immediate temporary solution. However, the problem was that the solution is shortsighted and was not able to be extended or managed correctly. Every effort afterward still remained a manual process in terms of updates and thus perpetuated a laborious effort to provide reporting and analysis—often missing the mark and intended goals.

Although this "solution" may have been the answer that time, and often is said to be temporary, unfortunately what happens is that it becomes the de facto standard: embedded in the workflow, the makeshift solution becomes the accepted process and practice for the department. The issues and questions of scalability, flexibility, extensibility, and manageability of the system begin to swell. In time, given the number steps to be taken to bring in data into the cube, the process became unmanageable due to the sheer volume of cubes that had to be individually created for each customization. To further complicate the situation, the report and analysis report were nevertheless provided, even though it was recognized that the data was neither complete nor accurate. The process was simply imbedded and locked into the department and its tasks. In other words, the temporary solution actually became the permanent solution for the department, and personnel were even allocated and assigned to continue and maintain it. This bad process was perpetuated and was allowed to continue, as no alternatives were known.

The unfortunate fact is that expertly designed and planned solutions would probably have taken the same amount of time to create and architect as the solution created without references to best practices. The ability to build a system quickly without any planning and design frequently results in a hacked system, built in a reactive mode, that seemingly providing an immediate solution. However, it cannot be a true solution if it results in the need to come up with yet another solution to solve its failures. Undoubtedly, the failure to plan and procure experts needed to build a complex system results in the creation of temporary systems that become problematic. Unfortunately, only after the problem becomes critical are knowledgeable resources or experts then called to cure and fix the problems that should have never existed to begin with.

Moreover, the project wasn't without faults beyond those that were IT-related. What sometimes plagues these projects is often either the involvement of many departments or the lack of unanimous support for the project (or both). In short: If you build it, they may not come. In the case of this study, there was no buy-in from the top business director. In fact, the project met with resistance all the way through, and the dissension trickled down to the point where the users began to resist the change. The most obvious lesson learned here is to ensure that support and buy-in are insured when undertaking a complex project. Support for the project ahead of time ensures some level of success when solutions are finally released. As BI professionals know, a great system can be developed and released, but without support for it, the system can easily be perceived as inadequate and useless. All methods must be used to circumvent results such as these; the issues can, in fact, be easily remedied by communication between stakeholders and expectations that are clearly defined at the beginning of the project.

Companies and departments that work with data have a need and desire to be able to handle access to data directly. But because access to the data is often not provided, the staff is left to come up with a way to provide the data for themselves. This need to work with data prompts workers to seek a tool such as a popular and readily available cube that will enable them to work with data directly, without the assistance and support of IT to properly model and build a supporting dimensional data model stored in a relational database management system (RDBMS). Without access to enterprise data and support from IT, departments often try to come up with some kind of system that allows them to do their work—or at least provide the perception that productive work is being accomplished.

10.3 The Resolution

With no idea of best practices to establish a proper foundation, the path to resolution begins with first recognizing and acknowledging a pain point. In situations such as these, where a tool and technology are improperly used and "stretched to the limit," that pain point may be that the current solution is no longer sufficient. What may have started off all right as a short-term solution now has outgrown itself to a point at which it can no longer be scaled up, extended, or managed. In many cases, the process of utilizing experts to execute the plan, instill best practices, and develop the proper solution for the organization may have been entirely dismissed.

With the pain point acknowledged, the process of developing the proper solution, complete with specific best practices in BI and analytics, can now begin. BI and analytical systems are data-centric and data-driven, and they take on an entirely different type of development that most application developers are used to. In data-centric development, the focus and central theme are being able to provide a data foundation which would provide complete, accurate, and up-to-date data for consumption and enabling downstream systems such as BI.

Data professionals with needed expertise and experience were brought in to create the data foundation with a design correctly architected and optimized for an enterprise data warehouse (EDW). The EDW provided a repository of cleansed and updated data that the department was able to access directly, replacing the process of updating customized cubes to do reporting. Although cubes were still preferred by the users, the warehouse is an entirely different proposition from using the cubes as a data store and the source of data for reporting. The new solution called for the most current data that had already been cleansed and updated through an extract-transfer-load (ETL) process to come from an EDW. With this process in place, the department staff could concentrate on reporting and analysis as opposed to acting as a pseudo-IT shop, trying to keep up with tasks and activities related to processing a data store.

Better reporting and analysis was provided via the EDW. Utilizing it accomplished a very important goal of having a single source of the truth. With this new data source for decision making, the company's BI environment was updated with the most current and modern set of tools and technologies for performing complex tasks associated with BI and analytics. In essence, in this case study, they went from doing things on their own with a tool they perceived as capable to actually having the most appropriate, best-fitting, modern BI and analytics tool as part of a holistic, comprehensive solution.

10.4 Summary

In today's market for BI, many tools and technologies are offered but they are often improperly used and "stretched to the limit" beyond for the intended use. What may have started off all right as a short-term solution often outgrows itself to a point where it can no longer be scaled up, extended, or managed. In many cases, the process of utilizing experts to execute the plan to instill best practices and develop the proper solution for the organization may have been entirely dismissed.

The BI space is currently experiencing this complicated—and unfortunately, common—challenge mired by choices and clouded by misinformation or lack of information. The use case scenario described in this chapter is a depiction of that challenge most relevant to this book; the authors suggest how to resolve the issue by focusing on the data foundation and proper utilization of the best fit tool and technology.

Chapter 11

The Prize for the Price: A Win–Win or Not

In This Chapter

11.1 Introduction

For decades now, various technologies and approaches have been tried, proven, and identified as clear best practices for building a complete, holistic Business Intelligence (BI) and data warehousing (DW) solution. Yet organizations still attempt to deliver a solution without reference to these best practices. Moreover, limited or no knowledge of how to approach development for this type of solution can result in omitting the vital, critical asset used for planning and the blueprint—if you will—for building a comprehensive, holistic BI solution. Overall, we call for adhering to best practices, seeking expertise for guidance, and planning accordingly when attempting to build these complex systems, so as to realize the prize and win.

11.2 The True Value of Expertise

This book was written from a practitioner's point of view, based on real, hands-on experiences collected through several decades of data warehousing and business intelligence projects. Organizations may dismiss the difficulties involved in building these complex BI and analytical systems and solutions. We've heard justifications such as:

- "It's just data."
- "We've done reporting before."
- "It's not rocket science."

All of these dismiss the complexity involved and, as with any attempt to deliver a specialized, complex solution, it is highly recommended that the assistance of a proven subject matter expert be sought—at the very least for guidance on the specific subject matter. Consequently, an expert can help navigate the waters and clear a path to success with a solid plan based on adhering to best practices and cutting out the noise. Simply stated, a BI and DW solution, because of its complexity, numerous moving parts, and components that need to be developed and coordinated, is not the type of project that can be easily delivered by a novice—even if the resource is experienced in a related area, such as software development or information technology.

To illustrate this point, consider an analogy: imagine that you need highly specialized heart or brain surgery, but the doctor who will perform your operation is a general practitioner. Or imagine being on a flight where the pilot is flying a different plane for the first time. No one would want to be caught in either of these scenarios; you would definitely attach a high value to expertise and clearly demand a certain level of experience and expertise, no matter the cost. So it goes when the success or survival of your organization is dependent on the successful delivery of the solution.

We have encountered, time and time again, attempts to create a complex BI and DW solution with no experience or guidance. As one might expect, this almost always sends organizations down a path that leads to rework later or, even worse, to a disaster in which nothing is delivered after a great deal of time and money is spent. So what approach can help avoid failure?

11.3 Data-Driven Development

The central themes highlighted in this book can be summarized as data modeling, data architecture, and the use of data as a common unified foundation and repository. It is obvious that best practice is to plan and lay out the data foundation first. Planning is the key to successfully implementing a data-centric application and data-driven system such as BI—because it is really all begins with the data. By taking the time to logically tackle the design and architecture of the data foundation, you can then plan and implement the system accordingly. It is similar to building a house: The foundation must be designed properly first and then built according to the design by the construction team. Without this attention to detail and process, the house may easily collapse. So it is with building a complex system, such as one for BI and analytics. For BI solutions, the data model is the blueprint to the system and is the vital key to a successful implementation.

To reiterate, our method and approach call for creating a data model and refining the data requirements from a conceptual data model to a logical data model, and finally to a physical data model. This is the dynamic process and mechanism that enable continual planning and design from the early phases and throughout. This extended review in itself can be considered a win simply because it doesn't commit any development resources and code before a roadmap and plan are solidified. Although it may seem like just one more price to pay in lieu of jumping in and coding, the review process actually saves time and resources that would have to be spent on rework for something that was not developed correctly from the beginning. What may not be obvious to the inexperienced is that doing it the wrong way almost always takes a lot longer (because of rework) than taking the time to properly plan and do it correctly the first time. Moreover, the process of modeling and architecting the data and putting it into a data model that captures the business requirements is essential. This vital and crucial process of translating business requirements into the right technical transformation and implementation is the basically the secret to our success—proven time and time again.

Overall, to ensure a win–win situation, we urge you to take the time to go through the exercise of logically modeling the data in your organization. The logical model will provide the "blueprint" and necessary understanding to build the right foundation for your downstream BI and DW solution or system. Atop that solid structure, you can then easily develop the application with confidence and clear thought. The resulting solution or system, specifically designed to meet your needs, is definitely a win–win!

11.4 A 360-Degree View of a Holistic Solution

Starting with a clear description of the business need for BI and the scope of a holistic BI solution, this book has covered the following topics as a best-fit pragmatics for the same:

1. The advantages and benefits of a logical data foundation based on the business processes involved, and how Oracle meets this goal through its products, solution suites, and tool sets. The key indicator is using data as a source to data as analytics.

   The analysis, evaluation, and selection of design criteria and key implementation specifics of the same, using Essbase for Analytical BI with OBIEE and the array of solutions based on it that help in complex multidimensional analysis. The continual integration of OBIEE with Essbase as an inherent component of it and why Essbase matters now more than ever as part of the total solution and strategy.

2. The use of OBIEE for self-service BI, Operational BI and Analytics in the real-world business realm, and how self-service BI leads the way forward for customer-based analytics and ad hoc querying.

3. The role of descriptive (what's-now), prescriptive (what's-next) and predictive (what-if) analysis, and how Essbase and OBIEE can be used for the same.

4. How the logical data model helps in extending and customization of Essbase by way of extending cubes and analytics that can be customized; and how Essbase fills the gap of predictive analytics that OBIEE lacks to a certain extent.

5. The semantic integration of Essbase and OBIEE, and using OBIEE as a data source for Essbase and its write-back feature to Essbase Cubes.

6. And last but not the least, the best practices of a holistic BI solution that is Essbase- and OBIEE-based.

No matter the solution to be delivered, it is the pragmatics of architecting a logical (dimensional) model and the related EDW in a ROLAP-based implementation augmented by Data Marts and MDX cubes that eventually is a win–win over all other solutions, and this book has repeatedly demonstrated this fact.

11.5 Summary

In this chapter we examined whether the recommendations forwarded in this book of using expert planning with data modeling and definitive utilization of tools could be declared and classified as a win–win. In addition, we try to illustrate the prize and advantage to the approach suggested in this book.

In the end, for creating a DW and BI solution, we declared that taking the time to plan and create a blueprint (in the form of a data model) is a priceless prize despite any perceived price attached to this approach. The data-centric expertise and planning are the keys to success and can help avoid undesirable results. Remember the old witty but very wise adage: "Fail to plan, plan to fail." As we have detailed in this book, that planning equates to the development of the blueprint in the form of a data model. This is our suggested mantra for all practitioners to live by.

Undoubtedly, the data-centric and data-driven approach proffered here with expert guidance and planning may require a price to obtain the prize, but nonetheless this approach can present a clear view and direction toward the right path to success; as such, it is a win–win.

Appendix A

Oracle Big Data and the Cloud for Analytics

A.1 Using the Cloud To Unleash the Potential of Big Data

Oracle has made tactical and strategic progress in Big Data and in using the cloud to leverage its potential. Big Data analytics can now be used in applications such as Business Intelligence (BI), predictive analytics, data discovery, cloud services, enterprise metadata management, advanced analytics, enterprise health care analytics, and the like. This appendix focuses on using the cloud to unleash the potential of Big Data and describes Oracle's role in cloud services and Big Data.[1]

Big Data Characteristics

The chief characteristics of Big Data are:

- Big Data includes structured, semistructured, and unstructured data across multiple sources.
- Six factors that matter are volume, variety, velocity, validity, virtualization, and value.
- From the typewriter to Twitter and everything in between, all consumer data is Big Data: random in nature and requiring presumptive analysis.

- Search and discovery are key requirements of enterprises as they navigate through huge volumes of Big Data.

Why Use Cloud?

A cloud-based solution:

- Delivers scale-out methodology for deployment of a unified platform from data to decisions, easily and efficiently
- Enables Big Data analysis, intelligence, and (new) analytics to fit into existing data environments with lower total cost of ownership (TCO) and faster time to value

The key is a unified platform for Big Data and all other data—a best-fit cloud-based solution—that provides high availability in the cloud and advanced analytics for all-data-as-a-service.

Essentially, cloud technologies can be used for Big Data in the following ways:

- Cloud-based self-service analytics—customized data-as-a-service solutions based on lines of business—let business analysts define and derive their own individualized Big Data initiatives.
- Cloud platform-as-a-service processes Big Data and all other data in a hybrid cloud in the right time (from definition to storage to transformation to integration) and pipelines it to a business analytics platform for customer-facing analysis and visualization.
- Enterprise search involving Big Data can scale to large proportions by using new or existing data discovery techniques, text analytics, and embedded search engines in the cloud on an as-is and as-needed basis.
- A cloud-based BYOD (bring-your-own-device) and multidevice connectivity solution can enable anytime-anywhere-anyone access to Big Data and its analysis by way of an authenticated mobile delivery platform.
- And last but not the least, cloud enables an easy and economic unified data access solution for both enterprises and small- to medium-sized businesses alike as social, mobile, and enterprise converge in the cloud.

A.2 Oracle's Role in Cloud Services and Big Data

As outlined on Oracle's web site for Big Data products and solutions,[2] Oracle's role in unleashing the power of Big Data using the cloud is as follows:

- Enterprise Big Data, which is the foundation for all data (structured, semi-structured, unstructured)
- Democratization or industrialization of Big Data
- Big Data management, using federated queries based on SQL that can query, Hadoop, RDBMS and NoSQL data sources (Oracle Big Data Cloud Service, Oracle Big Data SQL Cloud Service, and Oracle Big Data Appliance can be used to achieve this)
- Big Data analytics, Oracle Exalytics in-memory machine, Oracle BI Foundation, and Oracle Big Data SQL, which can foray into data discovery and advanced analytics and can be used for BI by way of prescriptive and predictive analytics and self-service analytics that can go beyond traditional and operational BI and analyses (data science can also be leveraged as part of this).
- Big Data integration for securing the Big Data lifecycle, which includes protection, data identity, traceability, and audit using Big Data Integrator, Oracle Golden Gate for Big Data, and Oracle Enterprise Metadata Management
- Using Big Data business aolutions that can drive insights into action based on the industry domain as a base

A.3 Beyond BI

Using cloud for Big Data can also make it possible for analytics beyond BI, such as:

- Going beyond BI: customer behavioral analytics, anytime and anywhere
- Zero-coding based Big Data analytics in the cloud
- Big Data discovery in the cloud for business analytics

References

1. Lakshman Bulusu, "Using the Cloud to Unleash the Potential of Big Data," DataSummit presentation, New York, NY: May 12–14, 2014.
2. https://www.oracle.com/big-data/index.html

Appendix B

Slides from Data Warehouse Architectures

B.1 Overview of the Corporate Information Factory and Dimensional Modeling

The following slides are extracted from a presentation by Rosendo Abellera for The Data Warehouse Institute (TDWI) that discussed and presented at a high level what were then the two prevailing architectures and concepts for building an enterprise data warehouse. The presentation was titled "Data Warehouse Architectures: Overview of the Corporate Information Factory and Dimensional Modeling."

Despite our current recognition of the apparent and proven advantages of one approach over the other, at that time, the industry was still trying to establish which one served as the proper way and best practice to develop and deliver data warehouse solutions. One approach was to go from the top down (popularized by Bill Inmon) and the other one was from the bottom up—from the lowest level of granularity(dimensional modeling by Ralph Kimball). Inmon and Kimball are considered the founders and pioneers of modern data warehousing (DW), for which Rosendo had built his DW and business intelligence (BI) career (from 1997) with the development and creation of his first DW and BI solution. From that beginning, Rosendo has architected and built more than a dozen DW and BI solution from the ground up for some of the most prominent names in business and government.

As it turned out, dimensional modeling prevailed by offering a method and approach that enabled the successful implementation of a DW and BI solution from the ground up in a timely manner. Incidentally, Oracle BI (or OBIEE) follows dimensional modeling. In terms of successful implementation, the bottom-up approach (Kimball's method with dimensional modeling) allows the most flexibility and the least amount of rework. The approach allowed for a series of incremental releases and "wins," as opposed to trying to release the whole data warehouse in one big bang or releasing aggregated or summarized tables and then having to revisit and extend them at a later time.

The presentation slides show and list the characteristics of DW and the differences between each approach. At one point, he suggests incorporating the best of both worlds by recommending initiating the project with a high-level approach to fully understand the entire enterprise, then shifting into dimensional modeling for implementation. Humorously, Rosendo called this collaborative approach as the Kim-mon approach—joining the names Kimball and Inmon.

The presentation culminates by properly categorizing the different characteristics to clearly distinguish each approach.

Introduction

Rosendo Abellera

▸ President, BIS3
  ○ Nearly 2 decades software and system development
  ○ 12 years in DW and BI space
  ○ 25+ years of data and intelligence/analytics

▸ Accenture

▸ Toshiba

▸ National Security Agency (NSA)

▸ US Air Force

Data Warehouse Architect:

❖ Comcast	❖ Mercury
❖ John Hancock Financials	❖ Lawson
	❖ Global Signal
❖ Manulife	❖ Diamond.com
❖ Engelhard (BASF)	❖ NationsRent

Other Notable Data Projects:

❖ LexisNexis	❖ US Steel
❖ ESPN	❖ British Telecom
❖ AAA	❖ Pfizer
❖ Staples	❖ Toyota
❖ Boston College	❖ Partech

BIS³

2

What is a Data Warehouse?

A data warehouse is a repository of an organization's electronically stored data designed to facilitate reporting and analysis.

❖ Subject-oriented
❖ Non-volatile
❖ Integrated
❖ Time-variant

Reference: Wikipedia

BIS³

3

Prevalent Data Warehousing Terms

Enterprise Data Warehouse BILL INMON
Corporate Information Factory
Data Mart Operational Data Store
Snowflake 3rd Normal Form
Dimensional Modeling Star Schema
RALPH KIMBALL Slowly Changing Dimensions

BIS^3 4

Which Approach Is Each DW Term Most Associated With?

Corporate **?**
Information
Factory

- 3rd Normal Form
- Bill Inmon
- Data Mart
- Enterprise Data Warehouse
- Hub and Spoke
- Operational Data Store
- Ralph Kimball
- Slowly Changing Dimensions
- Snowflake
- Star Schema

? Dimensional
Modeling

BIS^3 5

Overview of Two DW Approaches

▸ **Corporate Information Factory**

1. Top down
2. Data normalized to 3rd Normal Form
3. Enterprise data warehouse spawns data marts

▸ **Dimensional Modeling**

1. Bottom up
2. Data de-normalized to form star schema
3. Data marts conform to develop the enterprise data warehouse

6

Corporate Information Factory

▸ **Focus**
  ◦ Single repository of enterprise data
  ◦ Framework for Decision Support Systems (DSS)

▸ **Specifics**
  ◦ Create specific structures for distinct purpose
  ◦ Model data in 3rd Normal Form
  ◦ As a Hub and Spoke Approach, create data marts as subsets of data warehouse as needed

7

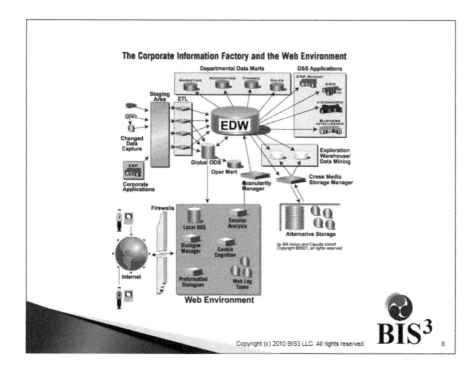

Dimensional Modeling

▸ Focus
  ◦ Business Process Oriented
  ◦ User Understandability
  ◦ Performance

▸ Specifics
  ◦ Declare the level of granularity
  ◦ Develop conformed dimensions
  ◦ Identify metrics and measurements
  ◦ Data Bus Matrix

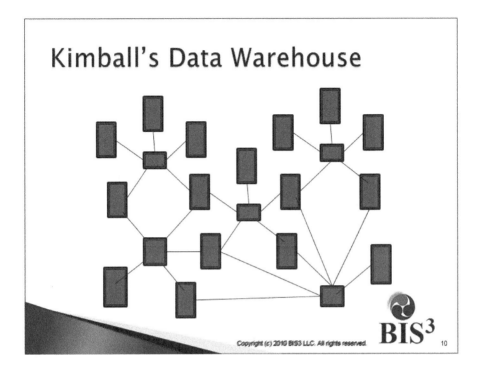

Kimball's Data Warehouse

BIS³ 10

Today's DW Landscape

▸ Popularity of Dimensional Modeling
  ◦ Adopted by ETL companies (e.g., Informatica)
  ◦ Evident in the strategies of mainstream BI tools such as Cognos, Microsoft's Analysis Services, OBIEE, etc.

▸ Shift in focus to Enterprise Architecture
  ◦ SOA and Master Data Management rethinking
  ◦ Consideration for Other Structures
  ◦ Combination of Inmon and Kimball Approaches

BIS³ 11

Kimball & Inmon Combined

- ▸ Holistic Approach to Enterprise Data
- ▸ Data Integrity and Cleansing
- ▸ DM in Semantic Layer of BI Tools
- ▸ ODS can be used as a great data source for the Data Warehouse

BIS³   12

KIM–MON Approach?

BIS³   13

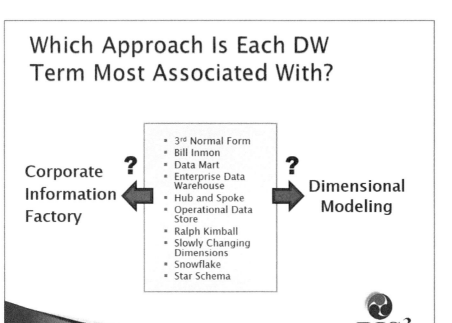

Which Approach Is Each DW Term Most Associated With?

Corporate Information Factory **?**

- 3ʳᵈ Normal Form
- Bill Inmon
- Data Mart
- Enterprise Data Warehouse
- Hub and Spoke
- Operational Data Store
- Ralph Kimball
- Slowly Changing Dimensions
- Snowflake
- Star Schema

? Dimensional Modeling

BIS³

14

A Data Warehouse By Any Other Name...

▸ Corporate Info Factory

- 3ʳᵈ Normal Form
- Bill Inmon
- Hub and Spoke
- Operational Data Store
- Enterprise Data Warehouse

▸ Dimensional Modeling

- Data Mart
- Ralph Kimball
- Slowly Changing Dimensions
- Snowflake
- Star Schema
- Enterprise Data Warehouse

BIS³

15

B.2 Slides from OBIEE 12c Presentation

The following slides were extracted from a presentation focusing on the differences between OBIEE 11g and OBIEE 12c. In response to the latest release of the Oracle BI software (i.e., OBIEE 12c), an analysis was done to determine some of the key points as to why one would choose to go straight to the latest version.

This situation was a "green field" and did not involve migrating any objects that might have previously existed. With that in mind, the presentation could focus on trying to determine whether there were any overwhelming differences and clear advantages provided by the latest version (OBIEE 12c).

Why OBIEE 12c Now

- Are there improvements to what was offered in 11g?
- Does it really have new features and capabilities that we need?
- Is now the time to switch to this new version?
- Is the organization ready for these changes?

Oracle Business Intelligence Suite Enterprise Edition

- 12c is essentially just the 2nd major release of OBIEE
- 10g was just a rebranding of Siebel Analytics

OBIEE 10g
2006

OBIEE 11g
2010

OBIEE 12c
2015

Considerations

Business

- **Performance**
- **BI Environment**
  - User Preference
  - User Intuitiveness
- **BI Capabilities**
  - Reporting
  - Analytics
- **Learning Curve**
  - Are users ready to learn a new system

Technical

- **Performance**
- **Hardware and infrastructure**
  - Powerful Servers
  - Cloud Architecture
- **Upgrade and Migration**
  - Additional Project
  - Dual Track
- **Admin and Maintenance**
  - Configuration and Setup
  - Improvements
    - OPMN / BISystemUser / GUID

OBIEE 12c

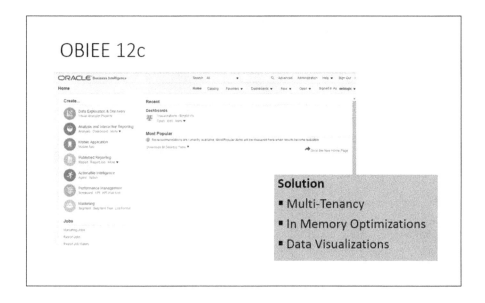

Solution

- Multi-Tenancy
- In Memory Optimizations
- Data Visualizations

OBIEE 12c Lifecycle Vision

✓ **Zero downtime**
- All system and application operations should be supported on-line
- No requirement for downtime of end-user functionality - Support offline configuration
- All system and application configuration operations should be off-line
- No requirement for runtime mid-tier processes to be started.

✓ **Vastly Improved from 11g Baseline Validation Tool**

✓ **Multi-Tenant**
- 12c will always be Multi-Service Instance (MSI) enabled
- Effectively 'Pluggable BI'

✓ **Self Service enablement**

What's New in OBIEE 12c

- BI Application Archive (BAR)
- System Cloning
- Backup Restore
- Disaster Recovery
- Multi-Tenancy / MSI
- Self-Service (SAC)
- Data Visualization
- Security Configuration
- Supportability
- Monitoring / Management
- Layered Customizations

Previously Very Manual Process

Steps:

1. Shutdown BI Server on the Source server
2. Gather following files from the Source server (onto a single directory on the machine to get them ready to copy over to the Target server):

	DEFAULT PATH	FILE(S)
Repository File	\Oracle\Middleware\instances\instance1\bifoundation\OracleBIServerComponent\coreapplication_obis1\repository	*.rpd
Web Catalog Folder	\Oracle\Middleware\instances\instance1\bifoundation\OracleBIPresentationServicesComponent\coreapplication_obips1\catalog	*.*
Config files	\Oracle\Middleware\instances\instance1\config\OracleBIPresentationServicesComponent\coreapplication_obips1	instanceconfig.xml
	$ORACLEBI/server/config/	*.*
	$ORACLEBI/web/javahost/config/	config.xml
.CSS files	$ORACLEBI/xmlp/XMLP/Users	*.*
	$ORACLEBI/xmlp/XMLP/Reports	
Other	(Customization files used for Dashboard, Writeback, etc.)	*.*

3. Copy files onto the Target server (onto a single directory used for staging the files.)
4. Copy files to respective locations within the Target server – reference the Default Path in above table for each set of files.
5. Update Target Connection Pool Settings to reflect the Target environment
6. Restart Target BI and Presentation Servers
7. Test

BI Pluggable

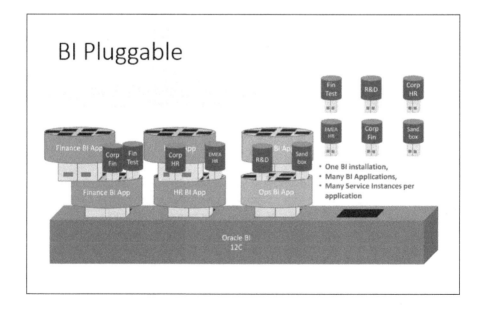

- One BI installation,
- Many BI Applications,
- Many Service instances per application

BI Application Archive (BAR) File

- Delivery artifact for a BI Application
  - Incudes webcat/bi server metadata/jazn for an application
- Application archive can be dependent on an another archive
- Multiple Applications can be deployed to a single BI Domain
- A Service Instance can be configured to choose an Application (BAR)
- A BAR file (Application) can be specified at Domain Creation (Install)

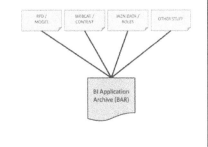

Oracle BI Validation Tool

Enables creation of a **baseline** set of data that is used for comparison with data from another environment

A way to perform **regression testing** on any two compatible Oracle BIEE environments
- Works within and across 11g and 12c versions

A way to instill **confidence** when performing an upgrade, migration or significant change to an existing environment

- Data verification
  Compare result output (i.e. actual numbers or text) from different versions

- Visual verification
  Capture screenshots of reports to check they are visually the same

- BI catalog verification
  Capture object and metadata and compare with the target system

- Logical query verification
  Capture logical query definitions and compare with the target system

- Performance verification
  Capture performance profile to check there's not degradation

Data Mashups

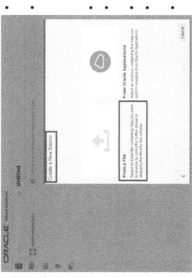

- Mashups – Fundamental Change in BI Server
- **Logical SQL extended to directly call external data**
  - Directly access external data in analysis
  - User uploaded files
  - Any source
- Just-in-time modeling
- Mashup across enterprise and user-defined data
- Private or shared access
- OBIEE embedded data store for user uploaded files
- Transparent caching in a database

Advanced Analytics

- Advanced Analytics - BI Server Built-in Functions
  - No external engine required
  - UI integration
  - Built in logical SQL
  - Leverages Mashups

- Custom Extensions
  - Define Custom Functions
    - Define inputs required from BI users
    - Provide execution script (for e.g. R)
    - Specify engine (R, Oracle Database, etc)
    - Use in Logical SQL

In Memory Analytics

- In-Memory
- **Visual Analyzer Mobile Data Mashups for Answers**
  - In-memory data sub-setting
  - MOLAP Acceleration
  - In-memory Indexing
  - Better scaling for mobile
  - In-memory personal data store
  - In-memory execution for mashups
- Optimized BI Server internal execution

Essbase in OBIEE 12c

- Embedded with OBIEE 12c – Finally!
- Builds structures based on Repository – LOGICAL MODEL
- BI Acceleration Wizard to suggest **Aggregation Strategy**

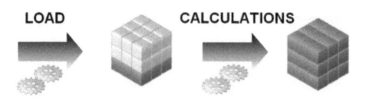

LOAD   **CALCULATIONS**

So Why OBIEE 12c Now?

- Does it really have new features and capabilities that we need?
  - ✓ *More integrated, holistic BI solution for enterprise reporting and analytics.*
  - ✓ *Big Data elements and capabilities with data mashups and advanced analytics*
- Are there improvements to what was offered in 11g?
  - ✓ *Major improvements for administration and maintenance*
  - ✓ *Improvements in Mapping functionality*
- Is now the time to switch to this new version?
  - ✓ *New era for BI - needs are prompting industry changes and improvements.*
  - ✓ *Second release for 12c projected for June 2016*
  - ✓ *Support cycle ending for 11g*
- Is the organization ready for these changes?
  - ✓ *Business Users have to learn a new system*
  - ✓ *Engineered system with hardware/software (i.e., Exadata, Exalytics, and OBIEE 12c)*

12c Or Not 12c. That Is The Question.

Pros
- Just one system to learn and maintain
- Easier maintenance
- Mapping feature "Easier and More Flexible"
- New Advanced Analytics and features for Big Data
  - Visual Analyzer

Cons
- 12c still new (11g stabilized)
- Less experienced resources available than for 11g
- Front-end development reliant on date of release
- Extra cost

Appendix C
Oracle® Data Sheets

Oracle Essbase

Oracle Essbase is the market leading online analytical processing (OLAP) server for enterprise performance management (EPM) applications. Designed specifically for business users, Oracle Essbase supports forecasting, variance analysis, root cause identification, scenario planning and what-if modeling for both custom and packaged applications. It can be tightly integrated with multiple data sources and the information generated can be delivered through a wide variety of reporting options. Engineered for scalability, security, and rapid-response, Oracle Essbase brings advanced analytics to the business user to enable greater understanding of the business, alignment of resources and improved business results.

KEY BUSINESS BENEFITS

- Supports a large user community across massive data sets
- Uses innovative, visual, easy-to-understand interfaces
- Facilitates understanding of customer segments and behavior patterns
- Enables rapid discovery of trends and highlights these trends in large data sets
- Delivers rapid batch load and calculation times
- Supports highly dimensional models
- Leverages investments in legacy systems

KEY FEATURES

- Move beyond silos of business intelligence and disconnected spreadsheets
- Real-time analysis of key customer data, finances and spending, and product profitability
- Cost-saving links to existing systems
- Speed-of-thought analysis for thousands of concurrent users
- Fast and easy development, deployment, and maintenance
- Robust security system

Richest User Experience

Oracle Essbase brings powerful online analytics processing (OLAP) directly to the business user. Query results can be displayed through interfaces of the user's choice, including Microsoft Office tools, and the variety of intuitive reporting options which Oracle offers. With the advantage of consistent, sub-second response times, users can interact with the data at the speed-of-thought without support from technical experts. This ability to "converse" with the data—understanding that an answer to one question leads to another—enables business users to better identify and analyze the metrics and relationships that influence performance, and to make better, more informed decisions. Users can share their saved reports, and modify their appearance, or create powerful additional queries as new questions arise.

Multi-dimensional Representation and Extension

Data is categorized in Oracle Essbase in the form of dimensions, a dimension could for instance represent a time period or a product or a customer. Thus a query may be to compare actual sales for a product in a specified state during the month of March 2010 with the corresponding budgeted value for that month. There are often relationships between members of a dimension and these relationships are represented by a hierarchy. A hierarchy enables mathematical calculations to be executed against the data, so for example all the sales for individual states can be aggregated to create a value for the entire USA. Oracle Essbase allows multiple hierarchies to be established so data can be speedily calculated or aggregated. Structures in Oracle Essbase such as dimensions and hierarchies are displayed in the "Outline", which is a graphical representation that enables authorized users to easily review and maintain structures as business requirements change.

Users can extend data by using metrics or drivers to estimate what results will be in the future. These driver metrics can be based upon history, trends or entered by the user. These forecasted results can be compared with actual results and the reasons for variances investigated so that more accurate forecasts may then be produced. Users can also create further scenarios where they may model for exceptional changes in business and be prepared for turbulent trading conditions through this "what-if" analysis. This assists fast resolution of business issues and for risks to be managed.

Most Highly Advanced Calculation Engine

At its core Oracle Essbase contains a high performance calculation engine with over 350 pre-built, out-of-the-box functions. This comprehensive library enables Oracle Essbase to scale from simple aggregations to complex, cross-dimensional allocations. Financial formulas of all types are included to support business model development. In addition, business rules can be created to manage complex calculation requirements using a spreadsheet-like syntax.

Reporting Options

A wide variety of users, from many departments, will want to use Oracle Essbase. Delivering the information to them in a suitable form is of paramount importance. Data can be delivered to Oracle Business Intelligence Suite Enterprise Edition and in addition presented through a variety of formats including interactive dashboards, financial and production reports, Microsoft Office and advanced data visualization tools. Each of these reporting options suits a particular purpose, but all use the same data, and common data definitions ensuring consistency across the enterprise.

Figure 1: Best-in-class interfaces provide meaningful insights for business users

Open, Scalable and Secure

Oracle Essbase can be populated through a wide variety of tools that allow it to access any commonly recognized data source; the data can then be combined into a single analytic view, so the entire enterprise can be consistently reported upon.

Many organizations have multiple, large data sources from which the data needs to be extracted. Oracle Essbase performance is unmatched, offering inherent capabilities to optimize data load and recalculate data sets so results are speedily available to the users. Oracle Essbase enables detailed analysis of terabytes of data for thousands of simultaneous users providing up-to-the-minute, dependable information. This high-speed analysis provides business users speed-of-thought responsiveness to manage performance in real time.

User scalability features such as caching, multithreading, partitioning, and cross-platform support enable IT professionals to use fewer servers to support many analytic applications and large user communities. Supporting 64-bit architectures, Oracle Essbase enables larger analytical models with shorter calculation times, increasing the potential size of analytic applications, and the number of concurrent users. In addition, its n-tier architecture provides connection pooling, load balancing, and automatic failover so IT employees meet service-level requirements. With its High Availability Services feature, Oracle Essbase delivers distribution of processing across multiple physical servers to increase application availability.

With the potential to support thousands of users accessing significant volumes of data, security is a priority. Oracle Essbase leverages the Oracle EPM system foundation's common authentication system offering both high level and detail cell level controls and the support of Group or Role based security models. In addition, Oracle Essbase supports Oracle Fusion Middleware security components like Oracle Internet Directory, Oracle Identity Management, and a single sign-on for Oracle Enterprise Performance Management Workspace.

System Maintenance and Deployment

Manageability features within Oracle Essbase drive down IT costs. These features include packaged business product management applications; J2EE; .NET development tools; certified enterprise resource planning/customer relationship management application integration adapters; administrative wizards; automated maintenance scripts; Unicode support; and reusable dimensions, hierarchies, and business rules. The open architecture also lowers costs to develop, deploy, and maintain by leveraging existing IT skill sets. In addition, Oracle Essbase supports efficient, automated backup and restoration of the database as well as lifecycle management that provides a consistent way for administrators to migrate applications and artifacts across product environments.

Oracle Essbase leverages Oracle's Hyperion Foundation Services and Oracle Fusion Middleware to provide a common platform of services upon which companies can create, deploy, and manage EPM applications in one place.

Powerful Visual Analytics
for the Entire Organization
Oracle Business Intelligence 12c

Analytics should be more than a mirror of the past. As a strategic practice, it offers the ability to understand what is happening in the moment, and help you predict where your business can go. Making analytics a strategic practice requires a strategic platform that serves the entire organization's needs—from the agility of visual analytics and self-service data discovery, to the power of an enterprise platform, including operational analysis at scale, security, reliability, extreme performance, and centralized management. Only Oracle combines this agility and power in a single platform—because you shouldn't have to choose between ease-of-use and world-class analytics.

Visual Analytics

Visualizing data makes analysis faster and easier, and makes insights more readily available to everyone across the organization. Data Visualization in Oracle Business Intelligence 12c (BI 12c) offers a rich consumer-style experience that is now common across Oracle's analytics portfolio. Additionally, the entire user experience has been streamlined, demonstrating Oracle's continued commitment to making analytics as fast, flexible, and friendly as they are powerful and robust.

KEY BENEFITS
- Stunningly visual and easy to use.
- Faster time to value, higher ROI.
- Radically simple install, upgrade, and management for lower TCO.
- Comprehensive platform, from self-service to advanced analytics to operational analysis at scale.
- Seamless analytics across Cloud and on-premises.
- Self-service agility in a central, secure platform.
- No modeling or specialized resources required for data mashup.
- Instant mobile, no extra work required.
- Voice-enabled—talk to your data.
- Analytics anywhere with full mobile authoring.
- Easy to extend advanced analytics.
- Direct access to Big Data sources.
- Faster in-memory processing.

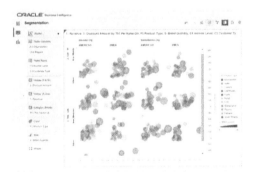

Figure 1. Oracle BI 12c Data Visualization sample analysis, highlighted trellis chart.

Visual Analytics

- Stunning data visualization.
- Secure sharing and collaboration.
- Intelligent highlighting automatically connects related data.
- Seamless user experience allows intuitive transition from discovery to dashboard.

Self-Service

- Self-service data loading, no modeling required.
- Self-service blending of personal and corporate data.
- Automatically inferred connection between data sets.

Mobile

- Touch and voice enabled, literally talk to your data.
- Full mobile authoring.
- Adaptive design for any device.
- Native sharing with other applications for both Android and Apple.
- Notifications on Android wear and Apple watch.

Advanced Analytics

- Integration with hundreds of free functions.
- Free R distribution for custom analytics, no RPD changes required.

Performance

- More in-memory processing
- In-memory Essbase on Exalytics

New Data Sources

- Direct access to Oracle Hyperion application data.
- Personal self-service data.
- Direct access to Cloudera Impala.

Easy Upgrade

- One file (BAR) for upgrade, backup, restore, recovery.
- Free Baseline Validation Tool

- **Stunning, smart visualizations.** Visualizing data is as easy as dragging attributes onto the screen. Optimal visualizations are automatically displayed based on the type of data selected, with no upfront configuration, and are also positioned automatically without requiring precise placement—so you get started analyzing right away, rather than spending your time configuring graphs, charts, and layouts. It's just as easy to adjust layout and change the visualization type, so you always have control over the display.

- **Everything connected.** Visualizations and data are all connected by default, which means highlighting data in one visual automatically highlights correlated data in every other, immediately showing new patterns. The overall experience is richly dynamic, with visualizations functioning as filters that work in combination with guided navigation and search, keeping your context and helping guide you through your exploration—much as you would expect in any online consumer experience.

- **Ease-of-use.** Updates throughout the platform blend ease-of-use and efficiency with powerful analytics capabilities. The interface for the homepage, Answers (ad hoc query and reporting), and Dashboards (analyses and dashboarding) has a simplified structure, more open space, and a cleaner approach to nesting and borders, helping you focus on the data and quickly see what's important. HTML-5 graphics improve view rendering and visualization display; and it's easier for you to create new groups, calculations, and measures, for simpler, more direct interaction with results.

Figure 2. Oracle BI 12c interface enhancements.

Self-Service

In addition to sophisticated data integration and modeling capabilities that power ongoing operational analysis, BI 12c offers new self-service capabilities for loading and blending data, with no modeling required—making fast analysis available to anyone in the organization.

- **Data loading.** You can now simply browse to personal text files and spreadsheets, then click to see a preview and upload them.
- **Mashup.** You can easily blend personal data with managed data—BI 12c automatically infers connections between data sets, as well as providing an intuitive user experience for redefining connections and creating new ones. Combining data sets gives you the ability to enhance existing managed subject areas by extending dimensions and adding facts, for increasingly timely and relevant analysis.

Mobile

BI 12c provides an increasing agile mobile experience that spans the portfolio, with the same mobile application on-premises and in the Cloud. Analytics are instantly available on any device, offer rich sharing and collaboration, and leverage the Oracle Mobile Security Suite for superior security, online and off.

- **BI Ask**. Now you can literally talk to your data with BI Ask, a search-driven approach to analytics that is optimized for touch and voice. Ask or type questions in search and see visualizations display in response.
- **Authoring**. In addition to full support for viewing (touch/swipe/zoom), full mobile authoring is available, using an adaptive design to deliver the best display for mobile devices. BI Ask results are an easy entry point for creating new visualizations and analyses, which you can flip through on your phone and tap to bring full screen for closer review.
- **Usability**. The interface for iOS has been completely redesigned and includes hand-off support for continuity across phone, tablet, and laptop; integration with Spotlight Search to help you find dashboards and reports directly from the Apple search box; and native sharing with other applications. Mobile BI for Android also now offers sharing and following for nearby devices, as well as the ability to project any dashboard or story to GoogleCast-enabled devices. Support for wearable devices is available for both the Apple watch and Android wear, which show alerts as notifications.

ORACLE BUSINESS INTELLIGENCE 12C

Oracle Business Intelligence 12c is the foundation of Oracle's complete analytics solution, available on-premises and in the Cloud for seamless analysis in any environment.

RELATED PRODUCTS

- Oracle Data Visualization Cloud Service
- Oracle Business Intelligence Cloud Service

Figure 3. Oracle BI 12c analytics on any device.

Easy Upgrade

BI 12c is a radically simple and robust upgrade from 11g, saving time and effort moving across versions. A single file, the BI Application Archive (BAR), includes everything necessary to backup, restore, test, clone, move, and upgrade an application. In addition, BI 12c includes a free utility to automate regression testing, the Baseline Validation Tool, which verifies data, visuals, catalog object metadata, and system-generated SQL across 11g and 12c releases. Together with architecture and lifecycle management enhancements such as modular metadata management; simpler, more robust security; and self-service capabilities, BI 12c streamlines platform management, significantly reducing the IT investment and delivering the lowest total cost of ownership (TCO).

Extreme Performance

Analyzing ever larger data sets requires extreme performance. BI 12c includes new options for sophisticated in-memory processing, to ensure fast response times across the spectrum of analysis.

- **Oracle BI Server**. BI Server in-memory optimizations deliver faster rollups and sorting, greater compression, and sophisticated memory usage for variable-length data, which translate to faster performance throughout the platform. In addition, BI 12c offers continued support for Oracle TimesTen In-Memory Database and is certified with the Oracle Database 12c In-Memory option.
- **In-Memory Essbase on Exalytics**. Extensive in-memory enhancements in Essbase on Exalytics improve concurrency, increase scalability through full utilization of Exalytics cores and memory, and provide significant performance gains by eliminating wait in background processing.

More Advanced Analytics

Predictive analysis is more tightly integrated, with expanded capabilities and an enhanced user experience that enable you to more easily forecast future conditions, group elements that are statistically similar, and expose outliers. BI 12c includes the ability to extend analytics with hundreds of function packages available for free in the public domain, and to run the free Oracle R distribution on BI Server. You can create custom R scripts, which can point to any engine (R, Oracle Database, Spark, etc.) without needing to change the BI RPD to deliver results.

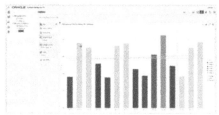

Figure 4. Oracle BI 12c advanced analytics sample showing trend lines.

New Data Sources

To address the ongoing availability of diverse new data and meet the growing demand to incorporate that data into analytics, BI 12c provides access to new sources, including both Oracle and Big Data (in addition to personal data, as described in the Self-Service section above).

- **Hyperion**. BI 12c supports extensive financial and enterprise management reporting and analytics through direct access to Hyperion Planning and Hyperion Financial Management application data, via single sign-on, native support for planning-specific logic, and automated full-fidelity model creation on metadata import.
- **Big Data**. With BI 12c you can analyze Big Data in Hadoop via Cloudera Impala. The DataDirect Connect ODBC driver to access Impala is included, and BI 12c generates Impala-specific optimized SQL queries for extreme performance.

Strategic Analytics for Higher Return on Investment

Oracle Business Intelligence 12c means you don't have to choose between ease-of-use and world-class analytics. BI 12c brings together visual analytics, self-service discovery, powerful operational analysis, reporting, and dashboarding, instant mobile, extreme performance, advanced analytics, easy access to diverse data sources, and more, in a single comprehensive platform that is easy to use and manage. You also don't have to choose between Cloud and on-premises, because BI 12c underpins Oracle's analytics portfolio, with shared technology, functionality, and user experiences, so you can build your analytics in the environment that is best for your business. This flexibility saves you time and cost, allowing you to focus on the value in your data and empowering you to take full advantage of analytics as a competitive advantage and differentiator, fueling innovation and increasing your return on investment.

ORACLE

CONTACT US
For more information about Oracle Data Visualization Cloud Service, visit cloud.oracle.com or call +1.800.ORACLE1 to speak to an Oracle representative.

CONNECT WITH US

 blogs.oracle.com/oracle

 facebook.com/oracle

 twitter.com/oracle

oracle.com

Integrated Cloud Applications & Platform Services

 Oracle is committed to developing practices and products that help protect the environment

Index